A CUP OF COMFORT®

for
Christian Women

A CUP OF COMFORT
COMFORT®
for
Christian Women

Stories that celebrate
your faith and trust in God

Edited by Colleen Sell

Avon, Massachusetts

Published by
Adams Media, a division of F+W Media, Inc.
57 Littlefield Street, Avon, MA 02322 U.S.A.
www.adamsmedia.com and *www.cupofcomfort.com*

ISBN 10: 1-4405-1118-7
ISBN 13: 978-1-4405-1118-9
eISBN 10: 1-4405-1176-4
eISBN 13: 978-1-4405-1176-9

Printed in the United States of America.

10   9   8   7   6   5   4   3   2   1

Library of Congress Cataloging-in-Publication Data
is available from the publisher.

This book is available at quantity discounts for bulk purchases.
For information, please call 1-800-289-0963.

For my Aunt Junella and my "sister-cousin" Cindy,
the dynamic mother-daughter duo
of Christian love and living

Contents

❧

Acknowledgments

In the creation of this book, I have been blessed with . . .

The contributions of the talented authors whose inspirational stories grace these pages;

The collaboration of the talented team at Adams Media—especially my "lady bosses," Meredith O'Hayre, the *Cup of Comfort*® project editor; Paula Munier, the creator of the *Cup of Comfort*® book series; and Karen Cooper, the publisher;

The love and support of my family;

The living example of what it truly means to be a Christian woman provided by Aunt Junella, my "sister-cousin" Cindy, my mother-in-law, my paternal grandmother, and others close to my heart;

And God's love and guidance.

Introduction

38 For I am persuaded that neither death nor life,
neither angels nor demons, neither the present nor the
future, nor any powers,

39 neither height nor depth, nor anything else in
all creation, will be able to separate us from the love of
God that is in Christ Jesus our Lord.

ROMANS 8:38–39

"Love" is one of the most frequently used words in the Bible,
where it appears thousands of times as both a noun and a
verb. Scripture after scripture reminds us of the love of God
and of Jesus Christ. But the Bible also commands us to love
one another.

The first scripture I ever learned, as a child of five or six,
is still my favorite: ". . . Love one another. As I have loved

you, so you must love one another." (John 13:34, NIV) Of all the scriptures, church sermons, and Sunday school lessons that have affected and guided my life, "love one another" has been at the forefront. In my mind, it is the root of all of Christ's teachings and of walking in His path, for we cannot harm and can only help what we truly love, in the way that our Father and His son love us.

When I reflect on the Christian women who have had the most profound impact on my life and on my faith, I realize that every one has been a living example of that simple scripture, *love one another as I have loved you.*

Coincidentally (or perhaps not), I found that same underlying message running through virtually all of the more than 1,500 stories that were submitted for publication consideration in this book. This Christ-like love for one another definitely runs through the more than forty personal stories gracing the pages of *A Cup of Comfort® for Christian Women.*

I hope you will enjoy and be inspired by these personal testimonies to the abiding love and amazing grace of our Savior, Jesus Christ.

—*Colleen Sell*

Air in My Tires

Mary C. M. Phillips

I need air in my tires.

I'm almost flat.

My bike, my adorable, mint-green Trek with the brown leather seat and flowered basket, is tough as steel and can handle the roughest terrain, but even she can handle only so much. Today, the tires need air. When the air is low, a heavy weight sets in and my bike rides differently—sluggishly, like a tired old tractor pulling around the weight of the world, and roughly, sending vibrations through my body with every bump I hit. When the tires are full, my ride feels great. I roll along, and I can take the hits.

It's amazing what a healthy dose of air can do for my bike—and for me.

Today, I needed some air, too. So I hopped on my bike and headed for Tanglewood.

I love riding my bike, even in a light rain. Know what the best cure for depression is? Driving through a big puddle!

I do all my errands on my bike. I used to use my car more often, but now my van sits in the driveway much of the time. On a nice day, only my bike will do, especially when my air is low—when I feel weighed down and deflated by the trials and troubles of life.

It's been a difficult week. So I need air today. I need to feel the rush of fresh air on my face as I cruise down the road on my bike. I need to get away from the house and feel alive.

I need air.

When my soul needs air, I read the Psalms. The Psalms are my spiritual oxygen.

So I head off on my trusty Trek, looking forward to pumping some Psalm air into my soul at the Tanglewood Preserve.

The ride to Tanglewood is about a mile. Most of the road is flat and freshly paved; there's only one hill, and it's not too steep. Once I get to Tanglewood, I plan to sit next to the pond and read the Psalms.

Today, I'm lucky. I get there before the residents of the nearby seniors home and actually get a bench to myself. With sweat on my brow, my kickstand in place, I sit on my bench with my adorable green bike by my side and inhale Psalm 25: 4–5 (NIV):

4 Show me your ways, O LORD,
   teach me your paths;
5 guide me in your truth and teach me,
   for you are God my Savior,
   and my hope is in you all day long.

Then I just breathe. I let God fill me up with His air—the Word, as air. And I pray for strength to get through life's pressures and for my loved ones and my community.

On the way back from Tanglewood, I stop at a local gas station and go straight for the air hose. Some gas stations now charge 50 cents to use their air pumps, but this air is free—like God's air.

I get my rear tire in place, remove the air cap, and attempt to fasten the air hose to the air stem—but I can't get a tight enough grip. After three unsuccessful attempts, I throw in the towel. I've actually made things worse, letting air out of the tire rather than pumping air into it, and now the tire is nearly flat. I'm in for a bumpy ride home. To make matters worse, it is so hot and humid that my clothes are now sticking to my skin. Frustrated, I hang up the hose.

Only then do I see the mechanic walking toward me and notice the look of compassion on his face. Without my having to ask, he takes the hose, untwists the caps, and refills my tires. Suddenly, both my bike and I are road worthy.

As I pedal down the street, the breeze cooling my body while the smooth ride calms my soul, I am struck by a realization: Sometimes I am incapable of filling my tires without assistance—just as I am incapable of filling my soul without faith in God. I cruise the last block home with the words of Psalm 23:1–3 (NIV) guiding, protecting, and restoring me.

  1 The LORD is my shepherd, I shall not want.

  2 He makes me lie down in green pastures,
     and he leads me beside still waters,

  3 he restores my soul.
     He guides me in paths of righteousness
     for his name's sake.

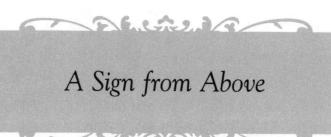

A Sign from Above

Joyce Stark

A few years ago, I attended a seminar entitled, "What would you do if you knew you could not fail?" The speakers were inspiring and entertaining, and the main point they made was that with enough belief in ourselves, we could eliminate the possibility of failure.

For a few weeks following the seminar, my colleagues and I were filled with single-minded ambition and determination. We addressed ourselves to our individual goals with great fervor, and in the weeks leading up to my vacation, I barely had time to chat with them. As I was leaving, Alison, one of the ladies I worked with, called out a goodbye and remarked, "You have been so busy, I don't even know the route you plan to take and the things you want to see this year!" The disappointment in her voice was so obvious that I felt guilty about having spent so little time with her since attending the seminar.

I had also skipped a few meetings of our local Writers Circle and a retirement party because I simply had more important things on which I needed to concentrate my energies. My husband also commented that I was less prepared for this vacation than usual and maybe having a break from work had come at the right time. I wanted to tell him that it was the reverse; it had come at a very bad time. But I bit back the words rather than cause an argument. Even on the plane on the way from Scotland to America, my mind was still full of the things I could achieve.

We landed in St. Louis in the mid-afternoon and decided to drive for a few hours and then stop for the night. We normally stick to highways, and fortunately for me, we were driving along one when I saw the sign: "What would you do for me if you knew you could not fail?" Naturally, the familiar words had drawn my attention to the sign.

But as we drove through the city, past the suburbs and small towns, and into the countryside, I began to realize what had happened to me, how self-obsessed I had become. I was focused alright, but in the wrong way and on the wrong things. You see, the sign on that highway in Missouri had two words that were missing from the title of that seminar: "for me." Those two words gave me pause and made me think. I began to go over all the things I would like to do for people if I knew I could not fail. Then I went over the things I would like to do for people even if I did fail.

I realized that I would never get success by being so singular in my pursuit of it that I cut myself off from everyone. The seminar had great gaps in it, like not mentioning how important it is to relate to people.

I glanced at my husband, concentrating on his driving, and vowed I would make this the best vacation he had ever had. I would do anything he wanted, go up things and on things and not complain about feeling dizzy or self-conscious. I vowed that when I got home, I would tell Alison and the others all about my vacation and make out a little journal for them, with photographs and leaflets, so they could share it a little.

That two-hour drive went by in no time as I went over a whole range of things I could do for people. I realized I didn't need focus and determination to do those things; all I needed was faith, but not only in myself.

We drove through parts of Missouri, Arkansas, Oklahoma, Kansas, and Nebraska, revisited Iowa, and ended up with friends in Galena, Illinois. Along the way, we stopped to see and experience many things, and I approached everything as if I were a representative for my friends at home, visiting on their behalf as well as my husband's and mine. Every night I wrote the day's events down in my journal so I wouldn't forget anything. I am sure this made us widen the kind of things we explored, because I wanted to share as much as possible with others.

Standing at the Lewis and Clark overlook at Council Bluffs in Iowa, my husband looked at me and smiled. "I think we have seen more diverse things on this vacation than we ever have before, and that is down to you. You seem to want to look at everything and anything this time!"

I smiled and knew in that statement that my re-think had been more than worthwhile. He was delighted that I was joining him in more activities and expanding my horizons. He was practically stunned to silence when at long last I agreed to go down the ski lift at Chestnut Mountain just outside Galena! Needless to say, I enjoyed it so much that I would do it again tomorrow.

On our last night in Galena, I lay in bed and saw the sign in my mind's eye as clearly as I had seen it alongside the highway that first day in Missouri. "What would you do for me if you knew you could not fail?" The name at the bottom of the sign read "Jesus."

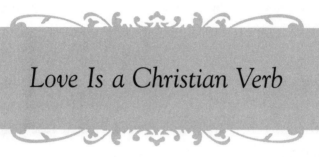

Love Is a Christian Verb

Priscilla Carr

My finest educator did not complete an elementary school education. She arrived in the United States at the age of nine unable to speak a word of English and began spinning cotton at the Amoskeag Textile Mills, in Manchester, New Hampshire. What lessons could this immigrant girl offer me? Marie D'Amours Cote was my mother's mother, and her indelible Biblical teachings sustain me yet.

When I was in third grade, I learned from observing Gran what she termed "charity of the tongue." Our downstairs neighbor stumbled into the hallway drunk, and I saw his son and his wife help him into the apartment. The next day I told my classmates and a few neighbors about it.

When Gran got word of my report, she said, "What an unkind and unnecessary thing to say."

I protested with, "I saw Mr. Maloney staggering. I saw."

The scowl did not leave her face.

"Gran, it's true," I insisted.

"Because you saw it, you had to tell? Explain how you showed God's love to this world by repeating someone else's misfortune? Because it's true you have to spread it like manure? How do you suppose it made young Michael feel at school? And little Maryann and Martha? Think about it, Missy."

As usual, Gran asked many questions and raised the name of God in the midst of things. As usual, her words gave me pause. I wondered, *What purpose did such gossip serve?*

When Gran spoke of a "Biblical tongue," she meant speaking of someone absent from the situation as if he or she were seated beside you. Following that instruction has made my life more enjoyable, more Christ-like.

Likewise, the terms "empathy" and "compassion" have taken on greater meaning for me as I've aged. Gran had both attributes in large measure. She used Christ's life as an example to teach me the Latin word "agape"—*to love without prejudice or motives of self-gain.* Not only did Gran define "agape" but she also lived it and emphasized that a Christian cannot live by faith alone, that one must do "works," as well.

Gran taught Biblical "charity of the loom." We sorted

scraps of corduroy and woolens from the mill and stitched and knitted them into caps, scarves, and mittens. We bought packs of RIT dye at Woolworth and dyed the dreary grays and browns to bright primary colors. While we loaded the cargo of charity onto a red wagon and delivered it to the poorest sections of inner-city Boston, Gran whistled and sang French nursery rhymes and smiled warmly at whoever answered each door.

"God is smiling broadly in this moment, Missy. How He loves a cheerful giver!"

Gran's "charity of the food basket" touched me most. We would forgo pies and cakes during the holidays in order to provide the widow next door with a turkey or a ham to serve her five children. I always loved buying those holiday meats and delivering them to needy family kitchens.

The grocer ridiculed us. "So what are ya, millionaires?"

Gran stomped her foot and said indignantly, "What a ridiculous idea! It doesn't take much, sir, to pass on some of our bounty."

On the walk home, though, she had a light in her eye when she said, "Girlie, though we haven't pies or cakes at our table, you are tasting generosity, and its sweetness will last you a lifetime. Remember, our Lord loves a cheerful giver!"

The smiles on our faces proved it, and I imagined God smiling, too.

When I was fifteen, Gran taught me the "charity of forgiveness" after I had spent the better part of a day sulking and moping. Over tea, I explained to Gran that my best friend and I had a bitter argument and were no longer speaking.

She advised, "Swallow your pride for her sake and for yours."

That girl and I recently celebrated fifty years as "best buds." We have supported each other through her husband's combat duty in Vietnam, the murder of a child in my husband's family, the birth of a handicapped child, marital crises, and the deaths of our parents and friends. I could have lost it all for the sake of stubbornness and pride.

On my college graduation day, Gran reminded me of my "charity of social responsibility." She advised, "Apply your God-given talents to the greater, common good. You have received many opportunities and with them comes a responsibility to create a better world."

After landing my first job out of college, I bragged around the neighborhood. Gran did not let it pass. She delivered my lessons on humility and class over a pot of tea.

"Miss, I would like to know why you believed it necessary to reveal your starting salary, which you very well realize is double what most folks around here are earning after years in a job?"

Stupidly, I went for it, "Well, to show what a good education can get you."

She was mute and unimpressed.

I dug myself in deeper. "I'm proud of my accomplishments and hard work."

Here it came: "Miss, did you ever consider how it might make someone else feel about themselves? About their situation?"

I hung my head and said, "I only thought of myself."

Then Gran gave me another definition I'd never forget. "The word 'class' is often misunderstood. It doesn't mean bigger, better, more, or exclusive. People who have class have the ability to make everyone in their presence feel good about themselves."

Silence followed as we sipped our tea.

Finally, Gran summed up with a homework assignment. "You are well schooled but not well educated, yet. In your fancy collegiate dictionary, look up the words 'crass' and 'boorish,' and then go to your Bible Concordance and read about the pride that comes before a fall."

When I was in graduate school, I realized Gran had taught me compassion and empathy in the tradition of Jesus, as in doing unto others as you would have them do unto you and in choosing to help those less fortunate. Countless times in her presence, the tenets of Christianity were put into practice. She didn't teach with diatribes or textbooks. It was on-the-job training, watching her do as she said, being known in the world as Christian by the way she loved and lived.

I never heard Gran speak an unkind word about anyone or reveal an unkind truth. She was the first at the widow's door with a basket, the first to lend a few dollars to someone out of work, and the first to patch up an argument. Such were my Scriptural lessons on how to evolve into a Christian woman. Gran showed me how to live biblically. I loved and admired Gran more than anyone I knew, and I still try to emulate her.

Marie D'Amours Cote died at ninety-six, weighing less than a hundred pounds and measuring less than five feet tall. We dressed her diminutive frame in a silver cross, blue linen dress, black pumps, a pill box hat, and spectacles and lowered her body into a plain pine box. I played "Amazing

Grace" on the trumpet, and my best friend sang "Ave Maria." The service was elegant, refined, and dignified—like Gran. The overflow crowd stood on the sidewalk in drizzle. Family, friends, and neighbors—along with professors, physicians, lawyers, and entrepreneurs whom she had kept house for—bowed their heads and wept openly . . . so immensely powerful is the effect of a Christian woman who lived the words of her faith.

Personal Hannah

Shawnelle Eliasen

I crept along the old, curved staircase, careful to stay in the shadows. It was three in the morning, and I was awake again. I skipped the stair step next to the landing. Our old Victorian home produced enough creaks and moans to wake even the soundest of sleepers.

I didn't need to be sneaking around, of course. I was in my own home. There was no danger of waking my husband, either. He was sleeping like a babe in our first-floor bedroom. Our five sons slept on the second story, and I was plodding up the stairs, in the dark, to my eldest son's room. I crept like a thief in the night because I was embarrassed to be making the journey again. It seemed like an invasion, to be standing above my man-sized boy.

I reached the top and tiptoed around the corner. Logan's room was messy, and I moved across the floor with trepidation. Books. Jeans. A tangled cord from the Wii system. I imagined what his dorm room would look like. The dorm room he'd be moving to in eighteen days. One day for each year that we'd raised him.

I stopped at the side of Logan's bed. The moon cast enough glow for me to see his features. Strong, straight nose. Wild mop of curly hair. Dark eyebrows that were more like his dad's than mine. Then I began my nightly ritual. "Lord, help me to let him go. I know that it's good. I know that it's right. It's just that he's grown so fast." I squeezed my eyes shut and wished that when I opened them he'd be a tiny bundle in blue flannel again. No. His six-foot-something frame still stretched beyond the end of his twin bed.

"Bless him, Lord," I whispered. "Make him strong. And guide me through this time, too." I tiptoed over a twist of yesterday's denim, crossed the landing, and made my way back down the stairs.

Raising Logan has been a joy. His temperament is much like mine: laid-back, reserved, gentle. I often joke that we'd been cut from the same cloth. But there are differences. Logan is funny. He has an offbeat sense of humor and a unique way of looking at things. His special qualities have always been uplifting, and he makes us laugh. I'd surely miss his joy.

I bypassed the hall to our bedroom where my husband still lay sleeping. Instead, I curled into a soft, leather wingchair in the corner of the living room. "Okay," I said in a whisper. "Time to count my blessings. One: Logan is healthy and strong. Two: It's a great opportunity at a very good school."

I was working on number three when I heard a whisper. In my soul. One word. It wasn't audible, but it came across loud and clear: "Hannah."

Hannah? I wondered. *What about Hannah? Who was Hannah?*

Then suddenly I understood and reached for the end table that stood beside the chair. I groped for the soft, worn leather of my Bible. Then I snapped on the lamp.

I knew where to find the story of Hannah. It was one I knew well. Hannah had struggled with infertility. I had, too, years ago. I'd clung to the story when my body wouldn't conform to our desire to have another child. But as I sat that night and read Hannah's story again, I was drawn to another part of the story. The ending.

Hannah had asked God for a baby and had promised to turn the child over to the Lord for His service. God heard Hannah's prayer and gave her a child named Samuel. Hannah fulfilled her part of the promise. When he was still a boy, she packed up sweet Samuel and delivered him to the temple. She still loved him. She still cared for him. She was still his mom. But she gave him over to God's care.

In the darkness, Hannah's story felt familiar. I'd asked God for Logan. I loved him with all the love that the word "mama" encompassed. Now it was time to turn him over. Just like Hannah. Sure, there were differences. Samuel was a boy. Logan was nearly a man. Samuel was going to be raised by a priest. Logan was going to college. But the bottom line was the same.

"I think I understand, Lord," I said aloud. "You're not asking me to let go. It's just time to turn him over to you."

No answer came. But I knew that I had understood. The silence that had been disturbing became a gentle peace. The darkness wasn't vast and scary. It was a quiet covering where a whisper could be heard.

I sat for a few more minutes. When, at long last, I felt sleep's gentle tug, I closed my Bible and reached for the nubby afghan from a basket on the floor. I pulled it to my chin and rested my head on the soft arm of the chair. I knew that I'd made the last desperate journey to Logan's bedside.

In the coming days, I'd help Logan pack his things. Like Hannah had cared for her son's needs, I'd fold faded jeans, plaid shorts, and Logan's Oscar the Grouch T-shirt. We'd fill gray, plastic totes and snap them closed with color coordinated lids. Then, we'd deliver him to campus.

My prayer had been to let Logan go. By guiding me to get up close and personal with Hannah, God had shown me that I didn't have to. It was just a matter of turning him over. I could do that. Because I knew that, like Samuel, Logan would flourish under His care.

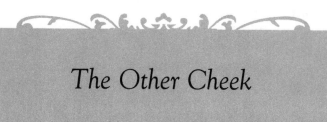

The Other Cheek

Nancy Brewka-Clark

Susannah took a faltering step toward me, her face tight with concentration.

"Good girl!" I held out my arms. "I knew you could do it!"

The only thing between us now was the metal frame of the walker. She took another step, and the little bell we had tied to it to keep track of her tinkled sweetly. Her pink velveteen sweatshirt was smeared with chocolate, and the matching pants had a big pucker on each knee from all the time she spent lying in bed on her side, adding to the impression of a toddler taking her first uncertain steps.

"Well done." I held the walker with both hands as my mother-in-law lowered herself gingerly into the wing chair by the fireplace. "Do you want the crossword puzzle?"

The words slurred. "Yes, please. Pen, too."

Sue-Sue, as all the grandchildren called her, had never used a pencil on the *New York Times* Sunday puzzle, and she obviously wasn't about to start now, despite her physical woes.

I handed her paper and pen. "Would you like me to make you some tea?"

Her blue eyes traveled to my face. Her mouth open, she stared around the room. For a moment, she looked all of her eighty-six years, the effects of the stroke pronounced in the vague blankness of those eyes. Then, as if a cloud had passed, she blinked, tightened her jaw, and pronounced, "You've been primping."

The word was so quaint that the accusation itself lacked sting. Before I could protest that I wasn't wearing a lick of makeup and never had, she lowered her gaze to the newspaper. "Dismissed," I said to myself.

I sank down on the couch and picked up my book, *The Seven Storey Mountain*, by Thomas Merton, the Trappist monk whose spiritual eloquence has touched thousands of lives. Like St. Augustine, he had led a colorful life before joining the priesthood. But I couldn't concentrate on the text. Instead, I found myself flicking little glances at Sue-Sue, her glasses perched on her nose, and wondered what was really going on under that thinning nimbus of white hair.

"Age-related dementia," the doctor had pronounced in the nursing home where she had been taken after a hip replacement. But all six of her children and their spouses privately disagreed. We were well into middle age ourselves, too old to buy into aging, itself, as a disease. Since Laura, one of her daughters, was a geriatric nurse, it wasn't long before we learned Susannah was being over-medicated. When the dosage was reduced, some of her mental acuity returned and Laura decided to bring her home.

Everybody agreed to help Laura out, but I had deep qualms. While Susannah and I had never clashed openly over the thirty years I had been married to her oldest son, I had spent many a bitter hour brooding over perceived criticisms. Sue-Sue's comments were usually delivered at a dinner table accommodating at least a dozen of her boisterous tribe. "She's a smart-aleck!" my husband would say. "Just give it back to her. She loves it." Since I had been raised not to squabble or exchange witty barbs, I suffered in sullen silence, gaining myself the nickname "Gloom and Doom." And oh how I hated it!

"About that tea." I put down my book. "Would you like it in here or in the kitchen?"

She shifted a little. "I have to go to the bathroom."

As she lifted herself up out of the chair, I thought of showing her how little I relished this task. It would be easy to make her feel guilty for being so helpless. All I would have to do is make one cruel little joke. Running through insults like a dim-witted standup comic, I entertained myself in silence as we made our way to the bathroom.

"I feel sorry for you," she blurted out.

"Me, too," I said, and we both laughed.

In the New Testament, the washing of feet is used as a sign of homage and devotion. Kneeling by Susannah, I felt a wave of tenderness wash over me as I cleaned her soft, creased flesh. Suddenly, I understood as I had never understood before the meaning of washing the less lovely parts of the human body: The humiliation of the recipient is reduced in proportion to the humility of the giver.

"Thank you," Susannah said, her tongue struggling around the added words, "I appreciate it."

I could have spoken volumes, telling her how much I appreciated all she had given me, but I settled on one phrase. "Any time."

That night, I woke up out of a sound sleep. My husband lay breathing quietly beside me. Thinking about the new intimacy between Sue-Sue and me, I wondered if she'd still call me Gloom and Doom. Instantly, I felt the familiar prick of resentment. Staring into the darkness, I thought about the endless ordeal of reaching toward a Heaven and a God and a Redeemer that even a saint in the making like Thomas Merton admitted sometimes seemed impossible to grasp. Then I thought of physics and the religious purity of a statement like, "Matter can neither be created nor destroyed." But I was no saint, and I certainly was no Einstein. What did any of it mean?

Finally, I got up and went to the window. Raising the shade, I looked out on the back lawn, bathed in a strange radiance that gilded the trees and grass. High in the sky, the full disk of a silver moon formed the center of a perfect cross that stretched its arms out as far as I could see. *This was just the way stars and lights looked when they were photographed*, I thought, *four brilliant rays streaming from a bright center.*

Perhaps the fine mesh of the screen was dispersing the light. Perhaps my mind, stimulated by the poetry of the Trappist priest, was producing an optical illusion. Never scientifically astute, my intellect struggled to explain it. I had nothing but a vague grasp of why my eyes might be interpreting this bright light as a sign of grace, of revelation.

My soul, however, simply sang.

The Life That Almost Wasn't

Sandy Adams

The young girl sat in the backseat of an unmarked police car with handcuffs cutting into her wrists. She was weeping uncontrollably and wondering how she could have let this happen to her. She had known in her heart that this was bound to occur. For weeks, she had tried to warn her husband and his so-called friends, but they had all laughed at her and nicknamed her "Ms. Paranoia." Yet, here it was—her greatest fear. As she looked out of the patrol car window, she saw chaos everywhere. Policemen, undercover officers, dogs, even the chief of the narcotics squad had shown up for a photo-op of the largest drug bust in the state.

Why? Why didn't I just leave? she agonized. But she already knew the answer. She had been kept penniless and drugged for weeks by her husband and friends as a precautionary measure, in case she chose to act on her paranoia and do something they deemed stupid.

As she looked around at the frantic commotion, she

saw a sight that was almost too painful for her broken heart to witness: Her three-year-old son was being restrained by a policeman and a social worker. She could see him fighting to get away and hear him crying, "Mommy, Mommy! I want my mommy." Why had she not done more to save him from this?

Unable to bear the sight of her precious little boy any longer, she looked away, closed her tear-swollen eyes, and prayed from the depths of her soul to a God she no longer believed existed: *God, if you are real, please take care of my baby. He deserves so much better. Find him a good home, where he will feel loved and be safe and happy.* Then she braved one last glance at him, knowing it would be the last time she would see her child, because she planned to end her own life as soon as possible.

Almost immediately after her prayer, the atmosphere of the whole scene began to change. She noticed the narcotics chief throwing things and shouting at his subordinates. Then, one by one, the police cars began to leave. Finally, the chief came to the squad car holding the young girl, unlocked her handcuffs, and told her to get out.

The chief was red-faced with anger. The police had been staking out the house for a month and had been issued a search warrant in anticipation of serving it the next day. However, due to suspicious activity at our house, the police were forced to act early and detain us while the search warrant could be brought to the location. For some reason, the search warrant could not be found. Without a search warrant, they could obtain no evidence, and without evidence, the case would not hold up in court. So just like that, the bust was over. No wonder the chief was enraged! Unfruitful for the police; life-changing for me.

Yes, I was that young girl. And I now had a second chance. I had my life back! I had my son back! And I was determined never to be in a situation like that ever again. Whatever it took, I would do it.

I grabbed my son, filled two suitcases with the few clothes and toys we had, borrowed some money from relatives, and departed as quickly as possible. I drove cross-country for five days in a rundown car to the safety of an old friend, while fighting drug withdrawal and trying to comfort a confused, frightened toddler. During the drive, I prayed constantly. I still wasn't sure if God existed, but I had no one else to call upon. As I remember those difficult days, I know my son and I would not have survived that long journey apart from God's loving watch care over us.

Now, because this story is true and not make-believe, I won't tell you that we lived happily ever after from the moment we escaped. Life was very hard for a while, as I struggled to make a go of it alone. Then, a few years after I'd come so close to losing my son and taking my own life, that dear friend who had given me shelter introduced me to the One who truly saved our lives, Jesus Christ. After I accepted Him into my heart as my Lord and Savior, the struggles lessened and my burdens grew lighter.

As I look back, however, I can see God's fingerprints all over my son and me during those difficult times—from the moment the chief's request for a search warrant was denied. It didn't matter that I did not believe in God; He believed in me, and He loved me right where I was. No one will ever convince me that it was not God who confused the administrative department during that drug bust, as an answer to a lost soul crying out in desperate prayer.

My son is now happily married with four beautiful children. As for me, I thank God every day for my life that almost wasn't, because if God had not responded to the desperate prayer of an unbelieving girl that day, I am certain I would not be alive today. God's magnificent grace and unconditional love have given me a new life filled with joy beyond measure, and I know that, as the old hymn says, "I live, because my Redeemer lives."

His Night Watch Care

Marsha Mott Jordan

My five-year-old grandson hated bedtime. He couldn't understand the concept of going to sleep when you still had energy left and hours in the day. One night while he was staying with me, I was unusually tired and eager to get some sleep, but Cobi was wide awake and resisting sleep with all his power.

"I need a drink."

"I need to go to the bathroom."

"I need my stuffed bear that I left downstairs."

He used every excuse he could think of to keep getting out of bed. After finally getting him tucked in, I went to brush my teeth.

Over the sound of the water running, I heard him call, "Gra-a-a-a-a-ma."

"What's wrong?" I called back.

"I'm too hot. Can I change into different pajamas?"

"All right," I agreed. We found some lightweight summer PJs with a big S on the chest. Of course, that meant he had to fly around the room a few times before leaping back into bed in a single bound. I kissed him goodnight for the second time and turned off the light.

No sooner had I walked back to my own room than I heard, "Gra-a-a-a-a-ma."

I went to see what the problem was. "My back is itchy. Can you scratch it?"

I scratched it. Then I tucked him in again and left the room.

Before I got to the end of the hall, I heard, "Gra-a-a-a-a-ma."

This time, we had to check the closet for monsters. After finding the coast clear, I pretended to lock the closet door and throw away the key. "Even if there were monsters in there," I said, "they couldn't get out now."

I'd barely turned off his light when the familiar call came again: "Gra-a-a-a-a-ma."

He was still too hot, so we opened a window and threw back one blanket. "How's that?" I asked with a yawn.

"That's good," Cobi said, "but I'm hungry."

Even though he'd had a snack before the bedtime ritual began, how could I send a starving child to bed? I'm a grandma, so what could I say? Downstairs to the kitchen we went. After a banana and a slice of cheese, I tucked him in *again.*

He was quiet for a good three minutes this time, but then he needed to get up and blow his nose. Then he needed his pillow fluffed up. And then he remembered that he hadn't hugged Grandpa goodnight. As I was tucking him in for the fifth time, he announced that he was thirsty again from the salty cheese.

"Now, Cobi," I said, fighting to keep my eyes open, "You can have one more drink and that's it. I'm very sleepy. I can't stay awake any longer. I need to go to sleep and so do you. If you call 'Grandma' anymore, I'm going to be upset."

He sighed, curled up beneath the blanket, and said, "Okay, Grandma."

Exhausted and ready for a good night's sleep, I fell into my bed. Then I heard a timid little voice from down the hall calling, "Mar-r-r-r-r-r-sha."

I couldn't be upset with him. I had to smile. I also couldn't really blame him for resisting sleep. Cobi has a passion for life and wants to squeeze every drop of enjoyment out of each day. His philosophy seems to be, "Play hard, laugh lots, and let the adults do the worrying."

Kids have the right idea. I should strive to be as innocent and trusting as they are . . . and leave the worrying to my Father, too.

That night, as I finally drifted off to sleep, I thanked my Father for His care. I was glad to leave all my problems in His watch care so I could rest peacefully. He can handle my worries, and He stays up all night, anyway.

This story was first published under the title "Night Sounds" in the author's book *Hugs, Hope, and Peanut Butter* (JADA Press, 2006).

Blessed Mothers

Nancy Antonietti,
as told by Frances Piscitello

I surrendered the pastry knife to Francine so she could cut my granddaughter's cake. "God Bless Nancy Rose" was written on it in a circle of pink sugar surrounding a white chocolate cross. The first pass of the blade sliced through white doves that flew at the edges and through pink frosting flowers that bloomed in profusion around the tall baptismal candle.

Francine was wearing a green A-line dress. She had taken to wearing that style as much to camouflage the fluid retention that resulted from her cancer treatments as to hide her post-pregnancy body. She was also wearing her new wig. I thought the style was a little unnatural, over-styled, but maybe only because I knew her so well, my beloved firstborn.

As Francine's face crinkled into a smile at a cousin's joke, my mind jumped to the day in the hospital, not a week ago, when I had realized what lay in store for us.

While my younger daughter, Rosanne, and my sisters

took over most of the care of Francine's baby, I kept vigil at the hospital with mine. When I entered the private room that morning, I'd found Francine in the adjustable bed, her eyes closed. The delicate skin beneath her lashes was tinged purple with fatigue, and my heart constricted as I gazed at her pale face. We were painfully aware that despite the chemo, which was causing her hair to fall out and her kidneys to fail, her tumor markers had been going up instead of down. I cursed this disease that was stealing my daughter from me. Children are supposed to tend their parents' graves, not the other way around. I was rummaging in my purse for a tissue when Francine opened her eyes.

"Hi," she said quietly and then smiled at me. She still had that beautiful smile, although the wattage had been turned down a bit, as with all her movements. I forced a smile to match hers.

She eased herself up to sitting, and I jumped to put the extra pillow behind her back.

"How is it today?" I asked.

"Okay. A little better. How's my baby Nancy?"

"Wonderful, just like you," I said. "Your sister Rosanne can't bear to put her down; she just loves her to pieces."

"Good," Francine sighed.

She hadn't been well enough to care for her own baby in the two months since she'd given birth. Masked by the symptoms of pregnancy, her cancer escaped diagnosis until it had spread so far that treatment was only a means to prolong her life, not restore it.

"Mom, they've got to let me out of here by Sunday," she said. "I have so much to do for the christening. I made a list. Where did I put it?" Francine pulled the bedside table closer to her and began rifling through the pages that littered its top. "It's not here." She got out of bed, and I resisted the urge to tell her to lie down.

"I have to find it," she moaned, as she rooted through the bag of personal things hanging from the back of the patient's closet. "I need to buy a wig, and order the cake, and—"

"I'll take care of all that for you," I said.

"Of course you will," she snapped. "You can do everything, and I can do nothing." The words hit me like a slap.

In the time it took to fill my lungs with the antiseptic hospital air, I recovered. She was tired; I understood. It was natural. I could take her sniping; that's what mothers did.

"It sounds like you know what you want," I said. "Let's make a new list. Tell me how everything should be."

After Francine dictated what she needed done, I moved on to the challenge of convincing the doctors to discharge her for the christening. Understandably, they were reluctant. Francine's primary oncologist told us that her tumors were not responding to the chemo and they were going to have to try to find a drug her cancer was not resistant to. He finally relented with the stipulation that she return to the hospital on Monday, when they would do a biopsy of the tumor tissue to try and match it to a different chemo.

Francine was thrilled to be allowed home for the weekend and seemed to shrug off the implications of the doctors' reports. I wished I could do the same.

The Mass at which Nancy Rose was baptized took place this morning. While the priest met with the parents and godparents at the back of the church, my husband and I walked down the aisle to sit in one of the front rows. The bright sunlight threw dramatic golds and ruby reds on the worn wooden pews. I reached out to touch the rigid seat back, craving a warmth that eluded me.

I made the sign of the cross, then slid in and knelt to pray. As I closed my eyes, I was aware of the mingled scent of burning incense and candles. With my knees pressed against the wooden kneelers, I prayed for health and happiness for us all but especially for this beautiful new baby and her mother. And I prayed for myself, that God would not take my twenty-two-year-old daughter from me just when her life was getting to the good parts.

Having baptized my own children in this church, I knew what to expect of the ceremony, and the predictability was calming. Francine and Carmen had chosen Rosanne to be Nancy's godmother and a cousin, Anthony, to be the godfather. The four of them responded solemnly to the priest's questions as he received Nancy into the Church.

In the sermon that followed, Father spoke about the significance of the symbols used in the sacrament. "Water is the most obvious symbol that we associate with Baptism, representing cleansing and growth, life and death," he said.

My focus snapped from Father's face to Francine's at the word "death." She didn't flinch, and I felt my lungs inflate, unaware that I had been holding my breath for her reaction until I felt my purse jab into my expanding ribcage.

Father's normally soothing words at the close of the Mass were a screaming reminder to me of my daughter's limited time. He bid us to observe the commandments of God "so that when the Lord shall come, you may meet Him together with all the Saints and may have life everlasting, and live forever and ever. Amen."

I stood motionless while everyone filed out of the church, lost in my thoughts. My daughter's tranquility as she strolled past me was an admonition. It was as if I heard a voice, spectral and loving, reminding me that if Francine could accept His will and live in the moment, I should strive to do the same. My eyes turned toward the statue of the Virgin Mother. That would be the best gift I could give them both on this day of sacrament. Humbled by my epiphany, I followed the congregation out with my head down.

Afterward, many relatives gathered at my house to celebrate the new life of Francine's dark-haired, chubby baby. My mother, the matriarch of the family, was ensconced in the living room with her cane by her side. Stooping first to kiss her, each of her children and their families filtered into every room on the first floor, teasing younger ones and trading news.

After a short break to digest their dinner, a crowd had reconvened in the kitchen for dessert. Those who couldn't fit into the room clustered at the doorway, peering over heads to watch Francine cut the cake. The other girls helped her pass plates, and soon everyone was enjoying the chocolate confection that had always been Francine's favorite.

While Francine posed for photographs with Carmen, the baby, and the new godparents, I took comfort in the fact that I had orchestrated the party just the way my daughter wanted, down to the smallest details on the beautiful cake.

On Monday morning, when it was time for Francine to leave the house and return to the hospital, I watched with tears in my eyes but pride in my heart as she gently kissed baby Nancy's forehead and handed her into my loving arms with the exquisite serenity of a blessed mother.

A Living Lesson

Monica A. Andermann

Carole Velm. Just hearing the name set all the little hairs on the back of my neck shooting up. I knew it wasn't right to find fault with any of God's children, most of all a fellow church member. But Carole could be so . . . annoying. I had never run across anyone quite like her anywhere, especially at my old church.

Earlier that year, my mother and I had decided to transfer our individual church memberships to a church closer to Mom's home. Now that my mother was getting older, attending church together seemed like the ideal situation. Not only did it give us an opportunity to worship together, but afterward it also gave me a chance to help Mom around the house or to take her on a few errands. I hadn't counted on meeting up with someone like Carole in the process.

Carole wasn't a bad person, exactly. She was just so dramatic. It seemed that as soon as our pastor rose from his seat to begin the service, Carole would breathlessly arrive at the back door, her aluminum cane clicking against the ceramic floor tiles as she slowly navigated her way down the center aisle to her favorite spot in the first row. Then there was the inevitable scene at the altar during communion when Carole would feel faint or dizzy in turns, requiring a member of the altar guild to run and fetch her a glass of water as the rest of the congregation waited to receive the bread and wine. And if Carole could make it back down the aisle after services without "almost losing her footing," she was sure to feel the effects of low blood sugar, sending the coffee social hostess scrambling to the fellowship hall to get her a jelly doughnut and coffee before she passed out cold.

Carole didn't simply require attention; she demanded it. She insisted on being escorted to the parking lot or the ladies room, reciting her inventory of health problems to whoever was unlucky enough to have been drafted to her service that week. So when my mother announced to me that she would volunteer to be Carole's escort, I was unable to mask my surprise.

"Why on earth would you put yourself through that?" I asked.

"She just seems like such a lonely soul," Mom explained.

Still, I didn't understand, and week after week I waited

at the curb for Mom as she listened for what seemed like an eternity to Carole's complaints. When the sun shone bright and sunny, Carole would huff and puff, claiming heart palpitations from the heat. In return, my mother would tell her how nice and rosy her cheeks looked under the warm sun. If snow was in the forecast, Carole was sure she would have a health crisis during the storm and no ambulance would be able to make its way to her house. My mother would just pat her hand, "Well, dear, then we'll pray that God will keep you healthy through the storm." One week after Carole rambled off a laundry list of aches and pains, my mother replied, "Praise God! All that pain, and you still made it to church."

The whole scenario seemed like a game to me, one in which I was the loser wasting valuable time that could have been better spent helping my mother with her own needs. So, when I spotted Carole at the supermarket after church one Sunday afternoon, I planned to head in the opposite direction. Quickly.

I tapped my mother on the shoulder and pointed in Carole's direction. "It's Carole Velm. If we move fast, we can get out of here without her seeing us."

My mother turned to me, "We will do no such thing.

She is a member of our church, and if she sees us, we will acknowledge her kindly."

I couldn't believe it. Mom had just spent a full twenty minutes in the church parking lot listening to the details of Carole's latest doctor's visit. Now she was going to waste more time with that woman. Well, not if I could help it. I pushed the supermarket cart around corners and down aisles avoiding Carole with all the skill I possessed. Mom and I completed our shopping and made it past the cashier without incident. I was about to claim victory when Carole spotted us in the parking lot.

"Oh, yoo-hoo! I forgot to tell you about the results of my blood test," she called across the asphalt.

My mother walked over to Carole and gave her another fifteen minutes of her attention. After Carole finished speaking, Mom made a brief reply, and Carole broke into a great, big grin.

"What could you possibly have said to make her so happy?" I asked.

"I told her I was glad to hear she's so prudent about taking care of her health so she could remain strong in the future. That way we could count on many more years of friendship."

I think my jaw hit the ground.

Mom winked at me. "Look, everyone deserves a kind word. Even Carole Velm."

Even Carole Velm? I all but gasped. Yet, when I drove out of the parking lot past Carole, I noticed her face was still shining. That's when it all finally made perfect sense. Didn't Jesus welcome all people with open arms? Didn't he instruct the self-righteous among his followers to do the same? Tax collectors, sinners, prostitutes: Jesus embraced them all with love. Carole was none of those things. She was merely a lonely woman seeking out the friendship of others in a different way than most. Regardless of Carole's methods, my mother responded to her as Jesus would have—with love.

I have to admit, I felt a bit ashamed in that moment of realization. Hadn't I, too, been a tad self-righteous when it came to my church sister? Inspired by my mother's Christlike example, I decided that from that moment forward I would be mindful to always respond to others with kindness—starting with Carole.

The next week I began to live out my lesson. Instead of waiting at the curb after Sunday services, I joined my mother as she escorted her friend to the parking lot.

"You know my daughter, don't you?" Mom asked Carole by way of introduction.

I reached out my hand to her, "How are you today?"

"This bright sun is burning my eyes," she said, fluttering her lids.

"Here, let's stand in the shade," I suggested. I examined Carole's soft, round face, "You know, in this light your eyes look as blue as the sky."

My new friend Carole broke into a heartfelt smile. And so did I.

Love Covers

Kathryn Thompson Presley

My husband proudly handed me his memory for my seventy-fifth birthday celebration. Although it is painfully written in his spidery scrawl, I am astonished at its clarity:

This is what I remember: My friend Cecil and I had gone to see Swan Lake, our first (and only) ballet at our college in Oklahoma. As we left the auditorium, I spotted a red head walking out ahead of us. I told Cecil (in a loud voice), "Man, look at that red head; I'd like to have that 'swing' in my back yard." She turned beet red and darted into the girl's gymnasium.

Later, at the Student Union, I saw her again at the soda fountain. I don't remember what I said, but she recognized my voice, blushed again and said, "There are some things you need to know about me: I'm Baptist, I don't smoke, drink, dance, or smooch and I intend to be an old maid missionary." The idea of her being an old maid was so ludicrous, I laughed out loud. She grabbed her drink and hurried away again.

Asking around, I learned her name was Kathryn Jane Thompson and she rented a room off campus from Mrs. Deen, my mother's friend at the Methodist church. It took some time and some persuasion from Mrs. Deen, but Kathryn finally agreed to go with me to a Valentine's banquet at her church. I don't remember how, but I finagled a part on the program and recited Browning's sonnet, "How Do I Love Thee, Let Me Count the Ways." I recited it directly to Kathryn. (When my mother had learned I was memorizing a POEM for a BAPTIST meeting, she told my Dad, "You'd better get out your tuxedo. There's a wedding in our future.") We were married four months later. That was 55 years ago last month. Signed Roy D. Presley

Roy watched my face intently as I read what he had written. As he wiped away my tears, I thought ruefully, *What a blessing he can't remember all the painful times in our marriage.* A series of strokes had erased most of his recent memory—the past forty years or so—but memories of long ago remained intact in the tangled corridors of his mind.

When we married in June of 1953, we were both equally naive and headstrong, a deadly combination. He was twenty-three, while I was still in my teens. We each had unrealistic expectations of what a good marriage should be, fully expecting to "get married and live happily ever after." It didn't quite turn out that way.

The first year was all right as we "played house" and got to know one another. But there were serious stresses even then. He was the youngest of four brothers and used to having his own way. I was the eldest of two sisters and accustomed to fixing whatever was wrong or at least trying to. Since he had no sisters and I had no brothers, we were both dealing with aliens.

They say couples tend to fight over sex, money, and/or in-laws. With us, it was always money. In the early years, when he was attending college on the GI Bill, we had no money to fight over. Then he graduated from college, the children came, and we had slightly more leeway for spending. That's when the serious quarreling began. Any time we had a bit of "discretionary money," I wanted to save it or buy something for the children. Roy had three major goals in life: to get a bigger and better bass boat, a bigger pickup truck to pull it, and state-of-the-art fishing tackle. He nearly always asked my permission to buy the boats, trying to persuade me what a good deal he'd found and how much the family would enjoy the new boat. I always said not just "No" but "Heck no!" He always bought the boat, anyway.

Had it not been for the children, I might have left him after the second boat, but I didn't have a degree back then, had no way to support my children, and they loved their father.

By the time I'd earned a degree and was making a decent salary teaching school, we'd been married nearly twenty years. So I stayed with him and simmered. There were still some good times; we had great joy in our children. For their sake, we went through the motions of loving each other. But on our worst days, I despised him for what I perceived to be his selfishness and immaturity.

He retaliated by criticizing everything I did—the way I looked, what I said, how I said it, the way I folded the laundry or loaded the dishwasher. It was impossible to please him. During those years, I often taught Bible classes about the "priority of forgiveness" but seldom practiced what I taught.

We were approaching our fiftieth anniversary when I awoke early one morning, studied him as he slept beside me, and finally admitted what I'd been trying to deny for months: The vascular dementia that had claimed his mother and her brothers was slowly destroying Roy's brain cells. Compared to this tide of misery about to engulf us, all our past disagreements seemed so trivial, so mundane. In the anguish of that moment, I forgave him everything, all those bass boats, all his petty criticisms, everything.

Now began a long, frustrating search for some combination of medications to calm him and to protect his remaining brain cells. I cared for him at home for several years, until a major stroke left him partially paralyzed. Then began the wearying task of finding the right long-term care facility. We were fortunate to find St. Joseph's Manor, but the cost was daunting.

The bass boat sold first, then the pickup, then our lovely home. I traded my Lincoln in on a Toyota; sold my first editions, most of our silver, and our coin collection; and rediscovered "poor" food: soup, beans, cornbread, vienna sausages. I bought a small garden home just a mile from St. Joseph's and walked to see him every day. He was always near the door watching for me, and his dear old face would light up with joy. "Well, hello, Darling!" His greeting never varied.

On his good days, he was almost normal. On bad days, he could not remember my name or that we were married. He proposed over and over again. "Honey, I've been thinking about this a lot lately, and I think we should just go ahead and get married." I didn't always have the heart to tell him we had been married over half a century.

I looked for ways to entertain him. He liked to watch *Jeopardy!* and *Who Wants to Be a Millionaire*. He could still answer many of the questions, smiling proudly at my praise. He had always been smart, and the left hemisphere of his brain seemed relatively unscathed.

We looked at family picture albums, and he recognized parents, brothers, grandparents, aunts, and uncles. But it was a mixed blessing. "Why don't they ever visit me?" he would ask querulously. If I couldn't divert him, he would demand, "Now, tell me the truth, Kathryn! Are they alive or dead?" Then the grieving would begin all over again for loved ones gone thirty years or more.

We frequently sat out in the courtyard in the Texas sunshine. Dementia patients often experience something called "sundowning," a state of increased agitation and aggressive behavior that happens late in the day. Sunlight seems to alleviate it. When the weather was really nice, we walked down to the pond and fed the ducks. He loved to throw bread crumbs to the silly birds. But he couldn't remember the ducks we had raised out on Lake Somerville. He had hatched them in incubators, fed them, and protected them from predators, then he'd taken the ducklings just off shore in a john boat and taught them to swim.

During those final years, he became my baby. I cleaned him, fed him, bathed him, shaved him, and diapered him. His attitude was, *Now, woman, this is more like it. What took you so long?*

During his last week, I felt his eyes following me intently as I puttered around his room. "Kathryn, could I ask you something?" His face was troubled.

"Well, we've been married fifty-six years, so ask me anything you want."

It took him a moment to frame the words, but finally he said, "Have you ever been promiscuous?"

I was dumbfounded. I didn't know he remembered the word; I was not sure he even remembered sex. Then I was angry. "Roy, you know I've always been faithful to you. How could you doubt that? What about you, have you ever cheated on me?"

He wrinkled his forehead, struggling to concentrate, and then declared. "Oh, honey, I hope not! I really don't think so, but you know my memory is all shot to pieces."

Later that day, he slipped into a coma. I sat with him and held his hand during the last days and nights. Just hours before the end, the hospice nurse reminded me that he might be able to hear us, even if he didn't respond.

I leaned over close to his good ear and whispered, "I love you, Roy Presley."

His eyes remained closed, but his face lit up as he answered, "I love you, Kathryn Presley." Those were his last words, his final gift to me.

His nurses all believed we had the great romance of the western world. And I was left to wonder what if. What if I'd forgiven him earlier and just loved him unconditionally? Could we have had the same delight in each other over the long decades that we had enjoyed during those last difficult years?

I don't know. But this is what I do know, what I share with the Bible classes I teach, and what I tell family, friends, and strangers on the street: ". . . love covers a multitude of sins, forgives and disregards the offenses of others." (I Peter 4:8 AMP)

We are all flawed, every one of us, so we have to forgive one another. To forgive, by God's grace, is to set a prisoner free and then to discover that prisoner was you.

The Test of Tithe

Heather Spiva

"How in the world is this going to work?" I asked.

My husband, Adam, and I were sitting on the sofa going over our budget for the second time that week. For me, this was a daily figuration by choice, because I was the accountant for the family. I had our monthly expenditures and income accounted for down to the penny—literally. And the way our finances looked, we had no wiggle room and no way to squeeze our pennies any more than we already were.

My husband shrugged his shoulders and subconsciously stared at our son's closed bedroom door. He had been sleeping peacefully for an hour, while we were struggling to figure where the money was going to come for the Christian preschool we wanted to send him to in the fall.

"Maybe he doesn't need that particular school," Adam suggested. "Maybe a less expensive one is just fine."

Those were ugly words to me, mostly because they weren't what I wanted to hear. Long ago, God had placed the desire in my heart to send our son to this specific school. In some ways, I felt like we were disobeying God not to send him there.

"I don't think so," I said firmly. "I really want him at the one we already discussed."

"We can't afford it. Where's the money for it?"

He was right. There was no money left in our budget. The scene was comical at best. We didn't have the funds for any preschool, let alone our choice school. That we were even having this conversation seemed ludicrous. But what about my desire to have him there; did it count for anything? Was I wrong for wanting something good for our son? While I knew God was faithful and I believed that he could provide for us, just as he had in the past, I couldn't see how this was going to work. I also knew that I might possibly have to do some soul-searching and relinquish my desire for our son to attend preschool at all.

I groaned and put my face into my hands. "He needs preschool," I said quietly. "Being an only child right now, I want him to interact with other children his age. This is what we planned on, years ago."

My husband watched me, and I could see he was torn. Torn because he couldn't provide what we needed, or even wanted. Torn because he was making his wife unhappy. Torn because he wasn't sure what to do to remedy the situation.

He took a drink of his hot tea, and I went over the numbers on my sticky note again.

"Maybe there's something else we can do," he said, raising his eyebrows in anticipation.

My head snapped back to him, my attention fully on his words. "What do you mean?"

"I mean, a way for us to be blessed. A way to get what was promised to us by God."

I hoped he wasn't referring to me working more hours. The reason we'd decided I would work part time was so we wouldn't have to pay for childcare. And what did he mean by blessed?

"I don't understand," I said. "I can't work any more than what I'm doing now, honey. And I don't want to burden my mother any more than we already have. Two days a week is enough right now."

"That's not what I mean," he said, frustrated that I wasn't getting it. "Remember the message last week at church about tithing?"

While I nodded slowly, my heart began to beat rapidly. Surely, he wasn't suggesting we tithe regularly, was he? While we had tithed when we could, we hadn't been consistent. Now, it seemed like the last thing we should do. How did it fit into the budget? Where would the money to tithe even more come from?

"We can't afford to tithe. We can barely make it right now," I blurted out before realizing what I'd just said.

Adam looked out the sliding door into the evening sky and shrugged his shoulders again. "Remember the verse in Malachi that says we're robbing God because we aren't tithing what's His to begin with?"

I felt defeated already. Who was I to say that we couldn't afford to give to God? God wanted us to give to Him not only because we, as His children, were supposed to honor Him, but also because He wanted to bless us in return.

"Yes," I said, sighing. "I do remember the verse."

Adam got his Bible from the other room and read the verse aloud: "Bring the whole tithe into the storehouse, that there may be food in my house. Test me in this . . . and see if I will not throw open the floodgates of heaven and pour out so much blessing that you will not have room enough for it." (Malachi 3:10, NIV)

He smiled and sat back down. "This means that what is ours is His. And if we give, as it says here," he said tapping the cover of the Bible, "then He'll bless us. I don't know about you," he said glancing at my notepad full of numbers, "but I think we could sure use a blessing right now."

Despite the verse, despite the fact that everything my husband was saying was right, I was still concerned. Naturally. Because now what God required most of me in this test was my faith. But did I have that kind of faith?

While the Bible verse made sense, the idea to give what we didn't seem to have went against every fiber of reason in my body—and against the numbers on the scrap of paper in front of me. But I decided it was worth a try to trust God and see what happened.

The next week, we wrote a check for the full ten percent of our gross income and went to church. With much trepidation, we dropped our check into the basket.

And we waited.

We waited for God to intervene on our behalf. We'd given money—God's rightful tithe—that we felt we couldn't afford to spare. Adam's employer had put a freeze on pay increases earlier that year, and I worked very little. How would we eat? Would the electricity be shut off? Would we have to sell a car?

Was God's promise of help truly in this decision?

That night in bed, I prayed. *Lord, we are choosing to obey you. We honor you through our gesture of faith. If you honor us financially, as the Bible says you will, then let this be a lesson to us for the rest of our lives to trust you always. Please listen to our prayer and honor our faith.*

I knew I couldn't solve the problem. I thought of a hundred different ways God could or would bless us, how the money might magically appear. My husband and I wanted to be confident; we wanted our faith to be real. But we also realized that in order for our faith to be activated, it had to be tested.

So we waited.

Two weeks later, my husband called me from work with a trembling voice. "I got a raise!"

My heart flip-flopped. What a miracle! The raise not only paid for our son's future preschool tuition, it also covered the tithe amount . . . to the dollar.

It seems so simple now. I wonder how we could've been so naïve as to obey some of God's commands but not all of them, and especially not this one—which had been the very impetus needed to grow our faith and bless us beyond our expectations. It was, in all ways, an act of God: good and wonderful.

Since then, we haven't once stopped tithing. God is faithful to those who are faithful to Him. All we had to do was trust Him, make the step of faith with our deed (writing the check), and believe. And it worked, just like He said it would!

A Mustard Seed of Faith

Galen Pearl

All the years my son James was growing up, I tried every possible treatment for his autism. I was a problem solver. I fixed things. If a treatment didn't work, then I simply moved on to the next, confident in my ability to ultimately find the right one: auditory training, sensory integration, behavior modification, play therapy, diet changes. Then there was the naturopath who looked me in the eye and promised me he could cure James—not just make him better, a complete cure. For months I put drops of various potions in water for James to drink four times a day. I kept daily records. I looked for any sign of improvement, finding great significance in . . . well, nothing. Each method held such hope . . . and led to such despair.

And I prayed. Oh, how I prayed. The Bible that said if my faith was as big as a mustard seed I could move mountains. I read the stories of healing. "Your faith has made you well." I read the stories of promise. "Ask and it shall be given." I asked for faith . . . for the faith to make James well.

If it only took a mustard seed of faith to move an entire mountain, then how much would it take to cure my son? What kind of pitiful faith did I have if I could not make him any better? I asked for more faith, better faith, worthy faith. But James was still autistic. Not only was I failing as a mother who could not help her child, I was also failing as a person of faith. I was so ashamed.

Then one morning I passed the partially open bathroom door as James was brushing his teeth. He was looking in the mirror and making faces and laughing. As I walked by, I heard him say with exuberant enthusiasm, "It's *great* to be James!"

I stopped in my tracks. All this time I thought it must be terrible to be James. And all this time he thought being James was terrific. In a stunning moment of revelation, I saw that James didn't need to be healed. I did.

The healing did come, but not right away and not in any way I would have expected or asked for.

When James was thirteen, he was in a special class for kids with developmental disabilities. One Friday afternoon I waited outside to pick him up after school. We were headed up to our cabin in the mountains for the weekend, and I was eager to get ahead of the traffic.

One of the teachers walked over to me and blurted out, "A terrible thing is happening to one of our students. Dan's father died a few months ago. Now his mother is dying of cancer, and there is no one to take him. He will have to go into foster care, but there is no foster family qualified to keep him because he is autistic. He will have to go to a residential facility."

As she began telling the story, I felt like I was inside a tank turret looking through the little rectangular opening at my future. The gears began clanking as the turret turned to aim in a different direction. I didn't want it to turn. I did not want to hear about Dan. In my mind, I covered my ears with my hands and started singing, "La la la! I can't hear you!" But I did hear. I heard the story in my heart and knew it was meant for me. I wanted my life to go on as it was, but my life could never be as it was because I had a choice that was not there moments before. My life would be forever changed no matter what I chose.

We went on to our cabin, and I spent the weekend praying. My prayers went something like this: "Dear God. No fair! Please don't ask me to do this. I already have an autistic child. I don't even know Dan. This is not my problem. You are mean. Why are you doing this to me? Please let me walk away." God just smiled and waited.

On Monday morning, thinking I had lost my mind and this was the craziest thing I had ever done, I called the teacher and said I would take Dan. In the next few days, I met with the social worker and with Dan's mother. She was a refugee from Vietnam and didn't speak English, but we spoke the same language. Like her, I was a single mother with a child who would need lifelong care. Like her, I lay awake nights worrying about what would happen to James if something were to happen to me. Through the interpreter I told her I would take care of her son. She looked at me, and I saw in her eyes a deep pain and understanding, as if to say, *You, like I, am the mother of a disabled child, and I am dying, so I am entrusting my precious child to you.*

Although we thought we would have several months to help Dan transition, I got a call exactly two weeks later that Dan's mother had been taken to the hospital for her final hours. I picked up Dan from school that afternoon. After taking him to the hospital to say goodbye to his mother, I brought a traumatized, grieving, autistic fourteen-year-old boy home to a new and terrifyingly unfamiliar family.

We were all so completely unprepared. I ran to the store for clean underwear and a toothbrush and made a bed for him on the floor until I could get him a real bed the next day. The social worker came by that night and certified me as a foster parent in emergency circumstances. And so our life together began.

Dan became James's brother and my teacher. He taught me about resilience as he coped with his grief and adapted to his new life. He taught me about creativity as his cooking and artistic skills blossomed. He taught me about respect as he lit incense to honor his parents. He taught me about communication as he made friends wherever he went, despite limited speech abilities.

Most important, he taught me about acceptance and forgiveness. Dan came to me as an almost grown autistic teenager. Although I advocated for him and got him all the services available to him, I knew he was pretty much the way he was going to be. By accepting and appreciating Dan just the way he was, I learned to accept and appreciate James just the way he was. And I forgave myself for the failure that had burdened my heart for so many years.

I guess my faith was as big as a mustard seed after all. I did move a mountain. The mountain was me.

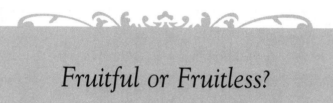

Fruitful or Fruitless?

Ellen Seibert Poole

"**M**om! The fruit is taking over your life!" blurted nineteen-year-old Erika. "You need to learn that you can't do everything."

It was the peak of harvest season but also the day to drive my daughter and all her stuff back to school at Seattle Pacific University, a three-hour drive from our home in rural Hockinson, Washington. Erika's possessions were piled by the door, ready to load in the minivan, but her crazy mother was still madly canning fruit.

"I'm almost ready. I just need to get this last batch of jars to come to a boil," I mumbled as I peered into the canner filled with quart jars of plum cobbler filling. "This old stove is so pokey! I'm sorry, honey. I didn't think it would take so long. But as soon as it's done processing, I'll take the jars out and we can leave."

"How long will that take?" asked Erika.

"About twenty-five minutes . . . after it comes to a boil."

Already discouraged that we had canceled plans to visit

her cousins on the way, Erika was now concerned that our other planned stop—dinner with Grandparents—would be compromised.

"I can't believe it," she grumbled. "This is so frustrating."

Yes, I thought to myself, *the fruit is taking over my life . . . and my sleep.* The previous night I'd stayed up until 4:30 A.M. putting up fruit. A mere three and a half hours later, I got up to pick, gather, and store more fruit, and then attempted to squeeze in one last batch of canning before we left. I knew that if I didn't deal with the fruit before departure, it would spoil while I was away. The previous day I had had to toss out two boxes of overripe pears that I'd saved for friends who had canceled their visit. Neighbors' horses and the compost pile appreciated the handout, but for me it was painful, considering the labor invested in picking and ripening them.

Although I looked upon our fruit orchard as a great blessing, I also realized it was a bit of a curse for one who cannot bear to see things go to waste. Perhaps it's my immigrant heritage or the "Depression-era mentality" I'd inherited from my parents and grandparents, but I've been unable to "just say no" to fruit. In addition, my recent transition from city to country life had created a fascination with the abundant harvest growing in my own backyard, compelling me to gather its bounty.

The refrigerator was so stuffed with fresh apples, pears, plums, blackberries, and raspberries that there was hardly any room for basics such as milk, eggs, meat, and cheese. I'd been giving away surplus fruit to everyone who would take it, but I still had several boxes of stored apples and ripening pears in my cellar, while mounds of windfalls cluttered my mud-room counter.

Our basement freezer was stuffed with apple crisps and plum cobblers, assorted fruit-filled muffins and breads, and various blends of applesauce. Alongside them were several plastic bags of whole berries and pitted plums waiting to be transformed into jam and other goodies, plus a large pot of mixed fruit sauce in "suspended animation" until opportunity arose to thaw and can it.

The cellar shelves were laden with an impressive display of Mason jars filled with colorful home-canned fruit, sauces, syrups, and jams—neatly organized in rows by category. Another assortment of recently processed jars sat on my kitchen table, waiting to join the basement collection.

Then there was the dried fruit stored in zipper bags on my kitchen shelf. All those hours of peeling and cutting bushels of fruit, only to have them shrink down to about 10 percent of their original volume after a day or two in the dehydrator.

Although I recognized my fruit compulsion, I still had difficulty tearing myself away to leave on our trip. While the jars finished processing, I filled up a cooler with all the fresh fruit I could cram in and loaded it into the car. I figured the more we could give away to relatives during the trip, the less I would have to deal with myself when I returned.

By the time we left that afternoon, my sleep deprivation had caught up with me and I was in no shape to drive, so Erika drove the entire stretch. I spent most of the trip dozing, but not without reflection. During a wakeful period, I apologized to my daughter.

"Erika, I'm really sorry that I've let myself get so busy with the fruit. You're right: It has taken over my life. I'm sorry we left later than planned and that we didn't have time to stop and see your cousins on the way up."

"That's okay, Mom," Erika said. "I'm sorry I was grumpy, too. I know you're making all that stuff for the family, and we really appreciate it . . . but sometimes you just try to do too much."

"I agree. I'm out of control," I confessed. "I'm sick of doing it—exhausted, in fact—but I just can't let it go to waste. I know there's some spiritual analogy here; I'm still figuring it out."

Our conversation turned to other topics, and we soon arrived at our destination. But I continued to ponder my fruit problem during the rest of our time in Seattle and even after I returned home. Here was yet another example of the Mary-Martha struggle within me, and unfortunately, Martha usually won out. I wanted to serve others and be a good steward of the resources God had provided, but my preoccupation with preserving the fruit before it spoiled caused me to miss out on opportunities to bear fruit in other ways.

My focus on the edible fruit had prevented me from serving my daughter with a timely departure and from spending meaningful time with family and friends. More importantly, I realized, it was crowding out time to sit at the feet of Jesus. I would plan to have my quiet time, but I'd get distracted along the way by the endless harvest calling to me everywhere I looked.

Paraphrasing Jesus' words to Martha in Luke 10:41–42, I envisioned Him saying to me, "Ellen, you are worried and upset about many things, but only one thing is needed. Choose what is better, and it will not be taken from you."

Okay, Lord, I hear you. Thank you for your wonderful provision of fruit in our orchard, but let me not forget that it is more important to spend time with the Giver than the gift. And thank you for speaking through my daughter to get my attention. Please help me to keep my priorities straight and to choose the better part—time with You.

Indeed, the fruit was a good thing, a blessing from God, but when allowed to get out of balance, it robbed me of what was most important: time with the Lord. This realization brought new meaning to John 6:27 (NIV): "Do not work for food that spoils, but for food that endures to eternal life, which the Son of Man will give you."

This story was first published in the June 10, 2006, issue of *LIVE*, a take-home Sunday school paper for adults.

A Perfect Fit

Jennifer Mersberger

P lease do this with me," my friend Sheryl pleaded. "It will be so much fun, I promise!"

As I sipped my steaming hot mocha, I examined Sheryl's sheepish grin. She loved taking on new challenges but always insisted on having the comfort of a good friend with her as she walked out on the ledge. Now she was cajoling me to join in on her latest endeavor: teaching a class of three-year-olds at church. With her southern drawl and mischievous eyes, Sheryl could sell ice cubes to an Eskimo, and I found myself cautiously agreeing.

Now, I have two kids of my own, but I have never been a teacher. Although I figured this was only babysitting a group of preschoolers for an hour or so each week, I was still really nervous. The first Sunday, I approached the half door with the "Cuddly Cubs" picture on it as if I were entering the lions' den. My stomach turned cartwheels, and my hands shook.

The childcare director talked quickly as she buzzed around showing that everything had its proper place.

"No questions? Good. You will do great!" she said as she handed me the neatly printed schedule for the day and was gone.

I hoped that Sheryl got it all down, because all I could hear was the sound of my racing heart pounding in my ears. Sheryl took it all in with easy-breezy confidence, while I stood rigid and clammy, forcing myself to appear attentive.

Before I knew it, it was time. The first set of parents came to the door with their son, Sam. I plastered on my best smile and went over to greet them. Sam took one look at me and instantly let out a high-pitched wail and latched on to his mom. I felt my hands trembling as I peeled the little tike off his mother while maintaining my picture-perfect smile.

"He'll be fine," I assured myself as much as Sam's parents. "We're going to have a great time, aren't we, Sam?"

The child looked at me as if I had a third eye growing from the middle of my forehead. Then he lunged into Sheryl's waiting arms.

"Aw, aren't you a sweetie pie!" she cooed. "I might just

need to take you home with me!"

Sam's cry was quickly replaced with a few giggles as Sheryl tickled his tummy and put him down to play with the toys. One by one, the kids arrived, each experience eerily similar to the first, with shrieking and crying at the sight of me being quickly replaced with smiles and laughter at the sight of Sheryl.

Once everyone had arrived, the real work began. The schedule demanded a craft, a Bible lesson, some kind of a skit with hand puppets, and a snack. I immediately assumed the assistant role, following Sheryl's effortless transition from one activity to another. The kids eventually warmed up to me, but they were drawn to her like bees to honey.

Snack time arrived an eternity later; we were in the home stretch. I graciously allowed Sheryl to continue captivating the kids with the Bible story while I prepared the snack: Goldfish crackers and pink lemonade. I've prepared snacks for my own kids a hundred times, so I knew I could do this. I felt my body relax as I busied myself with the preparations, running through a mental checklist.

Flower print napkins? Got it!

Twenty Goldfish crackers? Got it!

Dixie cup filled halfway with pink lemonade? Got it!

I displayed my hard work neatly on the small picnic table and eagerly awaited the kids' arrival. They were just on the other side of the room, but Sheryl had them so spellbound that I could have been juggling cats and they wouldn't have noticed.

When the story was over, the kids swarmed the snack table . . . but their buzz of chitchat quickly came to a halt.

"That's not how you do snack!" yelped Allison, the little redhead with big green eyes.

"Yeah, it's supposed to be on the ducky plates, Ms. Jennifer!" Sam informed me.

My heartbeat quickened again. What ducky plates? The neatly printed schedule didn't say anything about ducky plates!

The group was instantly whipped into a frenzy. How could such a tiny detail throw them into waves of mass hysteria? I scurried to find the elusive ducky plates. I frantically rummaged through the cabinets, found the plates, and switched the snack over. All was right with the world once again.

Parents arrived as the kids were still grazing on their snacks. One by one, we said our goodbyes. As the last mom arrived, I noticed she looked like she was carrying the weight of the world.

"Karen, are you okay?" I asked. "You look like there's something on your mind?"

"I'm okay; just tired, I guess. I feel kind of worn out from working and keeping up with Chase. I'll never catch up with it all."

"I know how you feel. I used to feel like that all the time, trying to get everything done. But I knew if I didn't change something, I would completely burn out. So I took a good hard look at my schedule and decided to say 'no' to a few things. It turned out great, and I realized I was the only one expecting me to do it all. I felt like I could finally breathe!"

"That's good advice. Maybe it's time for some changes. I think I know just where to start." Karen's face brightened as she scooped up Chase and said goodbye with a smile.

Week after week went by pretty much the same. I fumbled through the class as Sheryl sailed through the activities. The one thing I always looked forward to, though, was chatting with the parents, especially the moms. I began looking for ways to encourage them—a note, a Bible verse, a compliment, or even just listening to what they had to say. The pickup process went from one minute to several minutes as the parents stayed to visit with me. I made some great new friends.

"Girl, I don't know how you always come up with something to say to those parents. I'm glad I'm not the one who has to do it!" Sheryl said one day after class.

Her comment stayed with me for several days. How was it possible that the woman who wooed the kids would possibly be uncomfortable talking with the parents? And why was I so much more comfortable with the parents than their kids? I have kids, for goodness sake!

The sermon the following Sunday brought a much-needed moment of clarity.

"God won't choose for every person to serve the same way. Think about your body. Do your eyes do the same thing as your ears? Are your feet capable of moving like your hands? Each part has its own job, but none are more important than the others. They all work together so the whole body can function."

Not being comfortable teaching the little kids didn't make me a bad person; it just proved that it wasn't the right fit. God created me to minister to the moms. He created Sheryl for the kids. I was overflowing with joy and suddenly knew exactly what I needed to do!

The familiar feeling of anxiety washed over me as

Sheryl and I sat at the same coffee shop where it had all begun six months before.

"I've got something to tell you," I said.

This time Sheryl examined me over the brim of her coffee cup. "What's wrong? Is everything okay?"

"Well, yes, but you're probably going to be unhappy with me. I want to step down from the three's class."

"Oh, is that all? You really had me worried!"

"What? I figured you'd be mad at me."

"Girl, I know you only did the class to help me out. You didn't seem very comfortable in there, but I let it go because I really like being there with you. You should really think about going into the women's ministry. Those moms flock to you! I wish I could talk with them the way you do."

I couldn't believe my ears! I'd compared myself to Sheryl for months, and all the while she had compared herself to me. Our spiritual gifts were never meant to compete against each other; they were designed to complement each other. I couldn't believe it had taken me so long to figure it out!

I followed Sheryl's advice and began serving in women's ministry. God taught me so much, and His ministry began to flourish. That was eleven years ago, and I am continuously amazed at how God works. I'm no longer rigid and clammy, and now I am sailing through with confidence because I understand how God wants me to serve the Kingdom.

With God directing my path, I know this is a perfect fit.

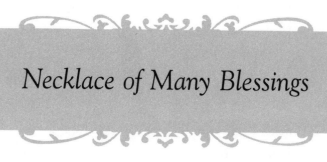

Necklace of Many Blessings

Lissa Stressman Smith

I had always appreciated the innate compassion and open-heartedness that my friend Bonnie exemplified as she interacted with every client at Christian Neighbors, no matter what their problems were. But when she told me she had presented the necklace I had given her as a birthday to a client, I felt angry with her.

For weeks, I had searched for exactly the right gift, and when I found it, I bought it for her even though the cost was much higher than I could really afford. It was a beautiful Silpada silver necklace that had a quarter-size pendant shaped like a scallop shell with the word "faith" written inside and a tiny yellow mustard seed hanging in the center. I was devastated Bonnie had thought so little of my gift that she had given it to a client two weeks after I had given it to her. I continued to seethe even when she told me she felt as though the Holy Spirit had directed her to give the necklace to a woman she had been helping.

Bonnie had known she wanted to become a nun years

before she entered the convent at age eighteen. She had been bullied and harassed throughout most of her high school years, but she always saw the best in everyone, no matter how unkind they were. Her child-like faith and deep desire to help others were the core virtues that had made her such an amazing Dominican Sister for twenty-two years. Bonnie's very being radiates an encompassing love that brings a gentle, unassuming quality to her spiritual endeavors.

Bonnie once confided in me the reasons why she had left the convent. She said she realized that the Lord was leading her in a different direction the last year of her life as a nun. At the time, she didn't know her new life would involve marriage and a career as an elementary teacher, but she knew she had to trust the Lord. Fortunately, her future would include a lay ministry that utilized all of the wisdom and compassion she had learned in the more than two decades she had served as a nun.

For years, Bonnie volunteered at Christian Neighbors during her summers off from teaching. Since retiring, she has continued to work at the agency full time.

Christian Neighbors is a social services agency that helps underprivileged clients with food, rent, heat, clothing, and a variety of other services. The unique aspect of Christian Neighbors is that the founder, Marie Johandes, structured the agency so that all of the staff are volunteers, including the administration.

When I first met Bonnie at Christian Neighbors thirteen years ago, we were immediately drawn to each other because of our similar attitudes regarding faith and our desire to help others.

I came to be involved with Christian Neighbors as a result of an assignment by my editor, Donita Hunt. I was working as a newspaper reporter at a small weekly paper, and Donita sent me to Christian Neighbors to cover their annual Christmas Party for disadvantaged children. I wasn't looking forward to getting up early on a Saturday morning to cover another boring charitable event. Little did I know that Saturday would change my life. The next week I started volunteering at Christian Neighbors, writing grants and training to work with clients as an intake worker.

Although I knew and respected that Bonnie's faith, compassion, and generosity guided her life, I was still upset that she had given away my gift. So while Bonnie smiled as she began to relate the story of the necklace to me, I continued to scowl. She told me she had never seen the woman she had given the necklace to before, that she was a new client at Christian Neighbors. Earlier that morning it had begun to snow, and near blizzard conditions were going on outside when the thin, bald woman approached Bonnie's desk. As the woman, Gail, began to tell her story, Bonnie knew there was a special reason why she had been sent to her.

Gail had been in an abusive marriage, and after her husband had beaten her up so badly that she required hospitalization, she had taken her two preschool-age children and gone to a woman's shelter. Through a grant-funded program, she had gotten an apartment, been provided with childcare, gone back to college, and landed a good-paying job working on campus in the lab. Gail had been so happy, and she praised God for the wonderful life he had given her.

She had only one semester left to finish before graduating when she began to experience digestive problems that were so severe she finally had to go to her doctor. Tests revealed she had stage-four pancreatic cancer. Unable to work or return to school, she moved in with her parents, who promised her they would take care of her children, but they were retired and living on a very limited income.

"If I had the faith of a mustard seed, I wouldn't be here," Gail said.

Bonnie was startled to hear that phrase, as she wore the necklace I had given her under her blouse, and Gail couldn't have possibly known that phrase was so close to Bonnie's heart—literally.

"I have lost my faith, and I am afraid I am going to die," Gail said as she began to cry softly.

Bonnie took off her necklace and showed it to Gail. Then she gently put the necklace around Gail's neck. "Now you do have the faith of a mustard seed," Bonnie said.

Gail left, and Bonnie watched as she started talking to another client in the hall. Soon Bonnie saw Gail take off her winter coat and give it to a young Hispanic mother who had just arrived from Texas and didn't own a heavy coat. Bonnie said she thought God had used the necklace to set off a chain of events that would bless numerous people and give Gail back her faith.

I felt ashamed as I said goodbye to Bonnie and got into my car to drive home. I had learned another lesson in my Christian walk, but I know that, just like every valley I have tramped through before, I will use in my life to bring about a chain of events to bless numerous people.

A Walking Testimony

Kathryn Lay

After more than three years beyond chemo treatments, I am still surprised when someone stops me, asks how I am feeling, and tells me how happy they are to hear that my lab results and doctor reports continue to be good.

Then they tell me how they prayed for me when I went through surgery and treatment. I can see the excitement in their faces and hear it in their voices. Sometimes they will press me about how I am doing, making sure I truly am doing well. They watch my face intently and leave me with a smile and a hug. There is a sense of relief in their eyes, a sense of joy that sometimes goes beyond my friendship for that particular person and leaves me surprised.

"I am so glad to see my prayers for you were answered," many tell me. I can hear the desperation in their voices.

Their love and concern is always a boost to my mental, physical, and spiritual growth. But sometimes the power of their joy surprises me. For a while, I didn't understand that my healing was important to them not only because they cared but also for another reason that was special to them.

I better understood how big a blessing my healing has been for these people who have held me in their prayers, however, after I read 2 Corinthians 1, especially verses 10 and 11 (NIV):

> 10 He has delivered us from such a deadly peril,
> and he will deliver us. On Him we have set our hope
> that he will continue to deliver us,
>   11 as you help us by your prayers. Then many will
> give thanks on our behalf for the gracious favor
> granted us in answer to the prayers of many.

When others tell me they are thankful that God has answered their prayers for my healing, they are also saying that God has given them hope. They prayed hard for me, and in seeing those prayers answered, they have been given hope for the things they are also praying for in their own life. When they praise God for my healing and see me at church with my family, enjoying life, doing ministry, it assures them that God can also answer their prayers for their own personal needs.

Reading 2 Corinthians 1:10–11, I realized, in awe, that I have become a walking testimony.

I don't often feel that I am saying and doing amazing things that inspire others. I don't speak eloquently and charismatically. I often wish that I were more like others who share their faith and spiritual knowledge to many through their exciting ministries.

But because of my road with cancer and the healing that came so quickly, many people who covered me in prayers now see a living testimony to God's promises whenever they see me. My very presence has become a reminder that God has answered their prayers.

I am also a living testimony to my friends who do not believe that God is there or that He cares for them. Their concern for me and their joy at my survival has opened many doors for me to share God's love and power.

These days, I see many other living testimonies around me: the young woman who returned to her family after running away to live a wild life. A saved marriage. The many whose illnesses have been healed. The father who got a better job after being laid off. All of these people are living testimonies to those who prayed for them. We can look at them and say, "Yes, God has answered our prayers," and our faith is strengthened.

Now, when someone asks me if I am still well, I know that they are also looking for hope in God's answers to prayers. I thank them sincerely for their prayers and walk away, strong in my own faith and a living testimony to theirs.

Bless These Reckless Drivers

Jennie Ivey

Seven o'clock in the morning found me sitting on the top step of my front porch tying the laces of my running shoes. The sky was a cloudless pale blue, and the sun was just peeking over the mountains that surround the beautiful Tennessee valley where I live. But I couldn't relax and take in the beauty. Because I knew the minute I set out on my run, my life was on the line.

Facing sparse but constant oncoming traffic, I walked for a few minutes and then broke into a slow jog. I hadn't gone a hundred yards before I had to scoot from the shoulder of the road into the high, wet grass beside it. A man driving a low-slung convertible was punching buttons on his cell phone. He never even saw me.

"Darn it," I muttered. "Now my feet are sopping wet." I turned in the direction the sports car was headed and hollered, "Hey, fella! Hang up and drive!" It was wasted effort, of course; he was long gone.

I began to jog again and was just picking up speed

when a red minivan crested the hill in front of me. The young woman at the wheel was twisted around, handing something to the child strapped in the car seat behind her. Again, I retreated to the tall, wet grass. Again, the driver never even saw me.

"What are you trying to do, lady?" I yelled as the minivan sped from view. "Cripple me?"

Once more, I began to jog. Five minutes passed. Then ten. Not a car in sight. I kicked it up a notch and glanced down at my training watch. Finally, I was approaching race pace. I looked up just in time to see the logging truck barreling toward me.

The truck was so heavily loaded with timber that it was hard to believe it could travel so fast. Through the windshield I could see the driver was holding a doughnut in one hand and a Styrofoam cup in the other. What was he steering with? His knees? This time I was certain that a couple of steps to my left wouldn't be enough. I dove for the shallow ditch that runs parallel to the road and rolled into it. Right onto the putrid remainder of someone's fast food lunch. Someone who liked ketchup a lot.

I picked myself up, scrambled out of the ditch, and shook both fists at the truck that was lumbering away. "Pay attention!" I screamed at the top of my lungs. "You could have killed me!" A thick, black cloud of exhaust smoke was the only reply.

Enough was enough. Even though I hadn't reached my usual halfway point, I crossed the road, turned around, and headed for home. Maybe my husband was right. Maybe I'd be better off running on a treadmill or at the high school track. I would certainly be safer.

Problem was, I didn't want to run in a sterile, man-made spot. Somehow, I felt closer to God when I was soaking in the wonders of his glorious creation. Fat livestock grazing in green pastures. Wildflowers gracing the roadsides three seasons of the year: ox-eye daisies, black-eyed Susans, purple thistle, Queen Anne's lace, goldenrod, Joe-Pye weed. Farm ponds teeming with ducks and geese and an occasional blue heron.

How dare these reckless drivers spoil my communion with nature! I steamed nearly all the way home. *But wait a minute,* I thought. *Aren't people God's creatures, too?* He made the guy in the sports car and the mom in the minivan and the man driving the logging truck. My anger wasn't honoring them. Or glorifying Him. It was doing nothing but dragging me down. Not to mention slowing down my running.

Pray for those who persecute you, the Bible says. It was worth a try.

The next morning while sitting on the porch step tying my shoes, I closed my eyes and bowed my head. "Lord, keep me safe while I run today," I whispered. "And bless all those who travel this road."

The man in the sports car passed me before I'd finished my warm-up walk. Not surprisingly, he was fiddling with his cell phone. *May his business prosper,* I prayed. *Or his social life or whatever else he's so busy taking care of.*

Halfway into the run, I still hadn't seen the young woman in the minivan or the guy in the logging truck. But while I watched for them, I began to notice something I'd never paid attention to before. Most drivers were obeying the rules—traveling the speed limit, both hands on the wheel, eyes focused on the road. A lot of them slowed down or moved over when they approached me. Many smiled and waved.

I smiled and waved back.

And I prayed. I prayed for the teenager obviously late for school and driving way too fast. *Lord, get her there safely.* I prayed for the farmer on his slow-moving tractor with a dozen cars backed up behind him. *Thank you for this man and the food he grows.* I prayed for the elderly couple whose heads were barely visible over the dashboard of their ancient sedan. *Traveling mercies to them, Heavenly Father.*

So it went. Mile after mile. Prayer after prayer. I reached my turn-around point, crossed the road, and headed for home. Not once that morning did I have to move from the shoulder of the road into the tall, wet grass, though I still have to do that every now and then. As a matter of fact, the man in the logging truck forces me into the ditch fairly often. But I don't holler and shake my fists at him anymore.

I just say a little prayer instead.

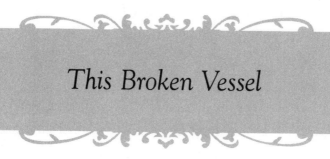

This Broken Vessel

Leann Guzman

God, I'm sorry, but I'm not here to worship you. I'm here because I need something from you, I thought as church began one Wednesday night.

It wasn't that anything horrible had happened. Rather, too many little things in life had begun to pile up, and I felt like the camel that had cringed under the weight of the straw. I was juggling marriage, two small children, a full-time career as an attorney, relationships with family and friends, my walk with God—all while nine months pregnant with my third child. Just one more thing would do me in, I was certain. It already felt like I couldn't keep all the balls in the air, and any day I was going to have a new baby, with all the demands and responsibilities and sleep deprivation that a newborn brings. How was I going to handle it all?

Lord, I need peace. I need strength. And I need freedom from feeling like I'm just not able to do it all, I prayed silently.

The praise team began to lead the congregation in

worship songs. But I was too drained to join them. How could I reach for God when I felt so empty? My simple confessional prayer was all I had to offer.

Then, during one of the songs, two words jumped out at me: "broken vessel."

Suddenly, I had a vision of me with my arms wrapped around a vase almost twice as tall as I am. The vase had been broken and was falling apart at the cracks. I tried valiantly to keep my arms wrapped around the vase, to hold all the pieces together, but my arms could cover only a small portion at one time. My arms moved quickly from one broken place to another, but some part of the vase was always left unprotected and vulnerable. It was just too much for me to hold it all together. Yet, even when it became obvious that I couldn't keep it together, I still felt that holding on with my two inadequate arms was better than letting go, because to let go would mean the vase would, without question, fall apart.

It didn't take the gift of Joseph to figure out that this was a metaphor for my life. I was trying to hold it all together on my own, but there was too much for me to handle. I couldn't do it all, but it felt that if I stopped trying, things would get even worse.

As I began to realize what it all meant, I felt God saying, *Let it go.*

I reasoned with my Lord: *But if I let it go, it will all fall apart.*

No, because I'll hold it, and my hands are big enough to hold it all and to hold you, too, so that neither you nor the vase falls apart.

I'd like to say I immediately let go and let God, but it took some moments of struggle. I had held on for so long that letting go wasn't easy.

But in that sweet way that God works, while I was struggling with His gentle command, our worship leader began to pray: "I surrender my job to You. I surrender my family to You. I surrender everything to You. . . ."

It felt like he was talking directly to me.

Then our worship leader said, "Someone needs to release some things to God." Immediately, I knew God was talking to me through my brother in Christ.

And so I surrendered.

I envisioned handing my broken vase to God and Him accepting and holding it in His arms. I saw him take what once was an ugly broken vase and turn it into a beautiful mosaic held together by caulk and mortar that wouldn't allow the pieces to fall apart. Some pieces of the mosaic were pretty and some weren't, which is a lot like the different pieces of me and my life. But all together, the way He placed the pieces, the finished product was beautiful.

Afterward, I felt such peace and release. I had asked God to free me from feeling like I wasn't able to do it all, and He had—though not in the way I had expected. I'd thought He would infuse me with strength and power, making me like a spiritual body builder able to carry all the burdens myself. Instead, He showed me that I don't have to do it all myself—that His strength is made perfect when ours is gone.

Now, when I feel like I have more than I can handle, I remember the broken vase that was bigger than me. I again envision placing it in His hands, this time without hesitation, knowing He'll take it from me and make the fragile pieces into a strong vessel—whole and beautiful in His caring hands.

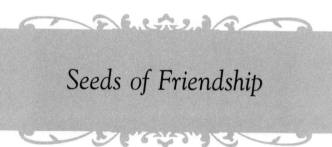

Seeds of Friendship

Stefanie Wass

Friendship: what a simple concept. My daughters, ages six and nine, are seasoned pros in this department.

"Mama, I made a new friend today!" boasts Julia, my first grader. "Her name is Hallie, and we hung out at recess."

The next day, as Julia hops off the school bus, another little girl waves wildly out the window.

"Who is that?" I ask. "Is she in your class?"

"No, she's in kindergarten," Julia smiles. "We just sit together on the way home."

Each day around 4:00 P.M., our kitchen phone starts to ring.

"Can Emily come over? I can drive her home if you can do the drop-off," the mom on the other end says, rearranging her busy schedule to accommodate our children's social lives.

As I grab my car keys, I start to wonder if I should spend a little more time on my own friendships. When was the last time I had coffee with a friend? Saw a good chick flick?

Had an actual adult conversation?

Like most young mothers, my life revolves around my children. Between driving my girls to piano lessons, Girl Scouts, and choir practice; making peanut butter and jelly sandwiches; and reviewing multiplication flash cards, I have little time left to cultivate new friendships. My work as a church and school volunteer is important, as is quiet time alone with my husband. But something is missing. An important piece of life's puzzle has slipped away, unnoticed until recently.

"This is Bring-a-Friend Month," the minister at church announces, causing me to squirm in the old wooden pew. "Everyone who brings a friend to Sunday service will receive a flower bulb. We'll plant the bulbs in the church courtyard and then watch our friendships grow."

"I don't even have any friends," I confide to my husband in the car on the way home.

"I know," he nods, "That's something we need to work on."

My old college roommate is my closest confidant, but her out-of-state address makes our visits infrequent. Of course, I've made acquaintances, like the moms I talk to at church and school meetings, but I tend to shy away from forging deeper bonds.

"A bunch of us are going out for lunch after Bible study," a young mom will offer, smiling warmly.

"Oh, I really shouldn't," I'll stammer, thinking of all the tasks that await me at home—piles of dirty laundry, toothpaste-encrusted sinks, empty cupboards hungry for grocery staples.

"We need another person for Bunco Wednesday night." My neighbor offered this olive branch recently while I stood outside waiting for my daughters' school bus.

As usual, I looked for excuses. "I'll have to check my calendar," I said. "I might be busy on Wednesday."

I admit to being fiercely independent and a bit of an introvert. My sport of choice? Lap swimming, where I splash away for a peaceful, uninterrupted hour a few times each week. My occupation? Freelance writing, a solitary job I complete in my quiet home office. My favorite vacation spot? A secluded Florida island, where I spend hours in a beach chair, my nose buried in a book.

Lately, though, I seem to be getting nudges to step outside my comfort zone.

"A family needs meals," the e-mail from church reads. "Julie has been rushed into emergency surgery."

I rally and deliver homemade cheese manicotti, feeling proud of my outreach efforts. At the door I am greeted by Julie's best friend, who is simultaneously doing laundry, feeding children, and cleaning the house.

"Wow, you're a great friend," I comment. Silently, I wonder who would step in if I were to fall ill. Who would care for my house and children?

"Bring a friend to church," the minister instructs. Judging from the already overflowing pews and crowded Sunday school classrooms, I know this isn't a plea for membership. It is, I think, a gentle push for community, a nudge toward togetherness.

I think about Julie and her best friend's selfless acts. If God wants us to care for each other, why have I been so antisocial and closed-minded? Suddenly, the void in my life seems real. But how do I go about making friends?

I start by calling a neighbor whose daughter is ill. Next, I make plans to visit my college roommate. Feeling bold, my husband and I even invite a couple to join us for dinner at a local Greek restaurant. Soon, invitations flow my way. Would I like to go to the movies? What about joining the neighborhood Bible study? Cautiously, I say yes, still feeling insecure but ready to take the leap—a leap of faith that friendship is God's will, a gift He wants for all His children.

A few weeks later, I'm standing outside my Sunday school classroom greeting parents as they drop off their first-graders. The father at the door looks like an old high school friend, albeit a few years older than I remember. His eyes catch mine and light up.

"Stefanie, is that you?" he asks.

"Jeff?"

"We just moved back to the area," my old friend grins. "Good to see you!"

"Your son is in first grade?" I marvel at my good luck. "So is my daughter!"

As Jeff and I talk, we soon discover that our children are in the same elementary school class.

"What a coincidence!" I remark.

But when Jeff tells me his new address, I know this is no fluke. His house is a stone's throw from mine. In fact, I can see it from my backyard.

This time, God has hand-delivered a friend to my doorstep. The seeds have been planted. Now, it's up to me to nurture them and watch them grow.

The Hobbyhorse Miracle

Debora Dyess

We woke up that morning knowing exactly how broke we were: no money in the bank or in our pockets, not much food in the house, and out of diapers.

"We'll just pray for a cash job," Steve assured me as he left for his garage. "That way we won't have to wait for the check to clear the bank. We'll be able to go to the store tonight."

I called the garage at noon, hoping for one of those jobs that pays well but doesn't take long to complete.

"I'm still praying," my husband's calm voice assured me.

"But, honey, it's Friday and—"

"And the day's not over. God will not let us down."

The kids and I ate open-faced peanut butter sandwiches for lunch, using up the last of the bread. I looked dubiously at the few remaining groceries, trying to plan creatively for their afternoon snack. I prayed for God's quick intervention before dinner.

At three o'clock, the kids and baby were still down for their naps and I had finished some chores around the house. So I placed another phone call to Steve.

"Anything?" I asked hopefully, truly expecting his enthusiastic response to fill the receiver.

"Nothing. . . ."

I could hear the office chair squeak as he shifted position.

"I mean, really nothing. No one has even come in the shop today. It's like working in a morgue, except I don't even have the dead guys to talk with."

After Steve and I prayed together and hung up, I prayed again: *God, I know what's in that kitchen, and so do You. If You don't want us to go without food this weekend, Steve has to have a job today. Even if it's just enough for some diapers and food for the kids, that would be okay.*

We had moved to Brownwood not long before. Steve bought a small garage here, and we'd relocated our family with great expectations. We found a tiny, cheap house in a poor neighborhood where we planned to live until Steve established himself in the community. We'd just started attending a new church where we felt welcome and comfortable. It had taken us several months to find the congregation and preacher we felt God wanted for us, but Southside Baptist had filled the bill.

Late that Friday afternoon, not knowing what I'd feed my children or use for diapers, I considered calling one of the women in my Sunday school class to ask her to pray with me. But I hesitated. I didn't know any of the ladies very well yet. Maybe I'd call later, I decided, if someone didn't come in to Steve's shop for a cash car repair by day's end.

When the phone rang at five, I smiled, thinking, *Here it is! Here is God's answer to our prayers. Steve was calling to tell me about the job God supplied at the last minute.*

"I think I'll keep the shop open an extra couple of hours tonight," he said instead. "Just don't give up. And don't stop praying."

"You haven't gotten any jobs?"

"Not one."

I felt my faith waver. "Oh, honey—"

"Don't stop praying," he repeated, interrupting the doubt I was fixing to verbally unleash.

"Okay, God—" I started praying aloud as soon as we hung up. But I stopped mid-sentence when I glanced out the window and saw a van pull up in front of our house. A man stepped out, straightened his three-piece suit, and started walking toward our front door.

In the neighborhood where we lived at the time, men in three-piece suits generally did not bear good news. I frowned and stepped out onto the front porch before he could mount the two wooden steps to the door. "Can I help you?" I asked cautiously.

"Hello." The man smiled and nodded. "Does that hobbyhorse belong to you?"

He pointed to a sad-looking, broken horse lying on its side in the yard. It had come loose from the springs a couple of days before. Currie, my four-year-old, had carefully tied a jump rope around its neck and played cowboy most of the morning, dragging the crippled hobbyhorse behind him in his imaginary rodeo.

Ah, that's it, I thought. *He's from the city and wants the yard cleaned up.*

"Yes, sir," I said.

"I'd like to buy it from you."

"Buy it?" I asked, confused.

"Yes." He laughed at the look on my face. "My wife and I restore them for craft shows. You know, repaint them, fix what's broken, and mount them on a pole. We sell them as indoor carousel horses."

"Oh." I said, relieved. "My Dad just bought my Mom one of those carousel horses. Maybe it was one you did," I smiled warmly. "You can have that one. I was going to throw it away in the morning, anyway. I'm glad someone can get some use out of it."

"I can't just take it," the stranger insisted. "We make pretty good money at this. It wouldn't be right to take it and not pay you."

I shrugged.

The man reached into his wallet, produced a twenty-dollar bill, and put it into my hands. "Thank you," he said.

I watched as he scooped up the broken toy and went to his vehicle. As he closed the van door, it suddenly occurred to me what God had just done. I rushed to the phone to call Steve, making a mental list of what the Lord had just supplied: diapers for the baby, bread, a couple of pounds of ground meat, milk, cereal for the kids. . . .

There was a tap at the door.

I opened it to the smiling face of the friendly stranger. "My wife says I made a mistake," he apologized.

I felt my heart sink. *Did he want his money back?*

"The horse is in perfect shape," he went on. "We won't have to do much at all to prepare it for painting. She wants me to give you another ten dollars."

I felt stunned and blinked back tears as I accepted the money.

"Are you a Christian?" I asked.

"Yes."

"Then let me tell you how God just used you." I told him the whole story—the desperate need, the anticipated miracle of a good cash job, the day-long disappointment. "Then you pulled up," I finished, "and God did our miracle in a better way than we ever expected."

"It gets better," God's messenger said. "We never drive down this road. Our son is a student at the university. He's a senior, and we've been coming to Brownwood for four years now. But today I took a wrong turn and we got lost. We got directions at a convenience store and were told that this street would get us to the campus. If I hadn't gotten lost, we never would have seen the hobbyhorse."

"Amazing," I smiled, reflecting on all that God had put in place to make this happen for Steve and me.

"Amazing is right," the man agreed. "I'd never even heard of Brownwood until our boy decided to come to school at HPU. He graduates tomorrow. He's a music major, and he plans on going into church ministry. He really loves it here, and I think he's a little sad to be leaving. He's directed music at a local church for the last two years and just really hates to leave it."

"Where does he direct music?"

Then the last piece of the puzzle fell into place as the man answered, "Southside Baptist."

Divine Intervention

Renae Tolbert

I yanked open the door and launched the words at my fifteen-year-old son. "We'll continue this in the morning!" We'd been arguing about a runaway girl Leon was dating, and now I was on my way out the door for a blind date with whom my friend Kathy had set me up. With my bad attitude lugging behind me, I slammed the door and stomped down the stairs to the carport.

My life was a mess. I was a single mom and a pack-a-day smoker. I loved bars and the lifestyle that accompanied the night scene. It was a comfort zone; I'd been raised in bars as a kid. Now, my son was going his way and I was going mine—but neither of us seemed to be heading in the right direction.

I arrived at the coffee shop, my nerves frazzled and definitely not in the mood for first-date dialogue. In a booth sat a thin man with a wiry, gray ponytail. I approached the table, and before I could speak, he asked, "You Renae?"

I plopped myself into the booth, resembling a spoiled

teenager. With a forced smile, I said, "Hi. Are you Larry?"

I hadn't wanted to go on this blind date in the first place, but for some reason, there I was. One minute I was fighting with my son, the next I was sitting in a restaurant across from someone I'd never met with a ponytail longer than mine. I thought to myself, *Kathy, what have you gotten me into?* I could not wait to call her in the morning. Battle number two was placed on the docket, right after my postponed battle with Leon.

After Larry and I exchanged the usual "how are yous," I wasted no time in telling him I had left mid-battle with my fifteen-year-old son to meet him. When I stopped complaining, Larry began telling me about how Christ could give me peace and direction in my life. He proselytized for two solid hours. Though I wanted nothing more than to shut him up and get out of there, I listened.

When Larry's sermon ended, I thanked him for the pie and coffee. Before we left, he asked if I'd like to go see *The Nutcracker* with him. I agreed because he said he had an extra ticket for Leon to go with us.

I drove home with new things on my mind. While wanting to reject all the "God stuff," I was curious. Something had drawn me to listen to Larry's preaching—and it wasn't Larry. It was something inside me that recognized some truth in what he'd said, and I wanted to know more.

Morning arrived, and I no longer had a score to settle with Leon; it simply didn't matter anymore. As for Kathy, I wasn't sure if I was glad or mad about the blind date she had set me up with. So I surrendered that battle too. I was on a new quest of my own. For now, I wanted to begin my search for this "truth."

I told Leon about my date with Larry and the conversation we had about God. The only thing Leon said was, "That's rad." I apologized about the blow-up the night before and asked forgiveness.

I began visiting the Christian bookstore several times a week. Not having the money or the desire to purchase anything, I sat on the floor and thumbed through Bibles, Bible studies, and commentaries. I looked up everything Larry and I had discussed. Though I continued to date him, it was not because I wanted a relationship with him so much as I wanted to find this "truth"—this peace, this "God" Larry promised was real and could heal my hurts.

Wednesday evenings, Leon went with a neighbor boy to a youth group at the church across the street. I thought the kids just got together and played basketball. I didn't ask questions about the youth group activities. However, I was concerned about some of his other friends from school, such as the runaway girl he hung around with. They were certainly a different group than the youth-group kids from the church. But I couldn't figure out exactly what it was that set them apart.

Larry seemed surprised that I didn't know more about God, considering I had a son who had been attending a youth group for over a year.

"Why would I know more about God?" I asked.

"Certainly they talk about Christ and pray at youth group," he said.

"He's never mentioned it. Guess I'll ask him," I said. Privately, I thought it was odd that Leon had not really said anything about what went on at youth group. We were like best friends; he told me everything. I couldn't imagine him not telling me about something as important as praying and discussing God.

The next time I saw Leon, I asked, "Do you kids pray at youth group?"

"Yeah," he answered, "but that's when I go out and ride my skateboard."

"Do they talk about Christ?"

"Yeah."

"Hmmmm" was the only reply I could muster.

Leon and I started talking more about God.

"Mom, don't get too into that 'God stuff,'" he warned me.

"Oh, don't worry. I'm not," I said. In the back of my mind, though, I wondered why he'd tell me such a thing.

The next Wednesday, he came home very excited. "Hey, Mom! The youth group is going on a trip called 'Urban Plunge.' They'll be taking food and blankets to the homeless and meals to AIDS victims. I really want to go, Mom. Can I?"

They left Friday afternoon. Two days later, when Leon got back, there was something different about him. He was so alive, so excited about the homeless people and people with AIDS he'd helped. And suddenly he was "into God." I didn't know what happened, but whatever it was, there was no doubt that my son was a changed young man.

Two weeks later, Larry and I had a heartfelt discussion. He asked me if I wanted to commit my life to Christ. We bowed our heads and prayed together. I asked Christ to come into my life, forgive my sins, and change my heart. Up until that evening, I was still hanging out in bars, drinking too much, and smoking those Salem Light 100s.

The day after I accepted Christ, I knew I would never go into a bar again. The desire was gone. A week later, I couldn't stand the guilt I felt every time I lit a cigarette. I felt as though I were slapping God in the face, inhaling poison after He had just saved my soul. I had read in the Bible that my body is the temple of Christ. Smoking just didn't feel right.

I stood in front of a mirror looking at myself holding that smoldering cigarette, and I prayed: "Jesus, if you really exist and if you really saved me, prove it by removing my addiction to cigarettes. I promise to break my habit of buying them if you will take away my addiction." After twenty-one years of smoking, I put out the cigarette and said, "Thank you, Jesus." That was in March 1992. To this day, I have had no desire to smoke again—God's proof to me that He did, indeed, save me.

I told Leon I had quit smoking. But he just shrugged it off. He had heard that promise so many times before.

Several weeks passed. One day Leon said, "Hey, Mom, you really did quit smoking, didn't you?"

"Yes, I really did," I said. "Now that you've asked, I'll tell you how."

I explained that I had accepted the Lord and made a commitment to live my life according to Christ's word. I explained how I prayed that the Lord would deliver me from smoking. I told him I had become a Christian.

Leon looked stunned. But not more stunned than I must have looked when he then said, "I did, too!"

"What? Why didn't you tell me?" I asked.

He explained that because he'd told me not to get too into that "God stuff," he was afraid to admit he'd become a Christian. With the "truth" now revealed, we rejoiced together.

The next Sunday, I went to the church where Leon had been spending his Wednesday evenings. I joined the choir, Leon got involved in the youth choir, and our lives were completely sold out to God.

I soon realized that Larry talked a good talk but did not walk the good walk. He dabbled in drugs and drank a lot. I found him to be cruel and verbally abusive to his children. When I began walking with Christ and questioned some of this behavior, he quit talking about Christ. We no longer had much in common.

Eighteen years later, Leon is married and the father of two beautiful boys that he and his wife are raising up in the

Lord. I am now married to the man God had been preparing me for all these years.

I am convinced that God knew that if he had sent me a man who was walking the walk before I was ready, I wouldn't have been interested in that "God stuff." The Lord met me exactly where I was at the time—and rescued both me and my son. It was an amazing orchestration of God's love, provision, and faithfulness. And I know He is not done with me yet.

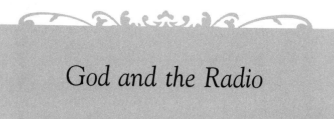

God and the Radio

Mitsie McKellick

It's February, and the man behind the desk is saying the chances are good that my son will probably die before he reaches his second birthday. That's eight months away. I open my eyes wide. I am feigning ignorance, pretending I haven't heard correctly. But I have. My throat is tight. Spit has pooled up behind my bottom teeth, and I can't swallow. I am weirdly pleased that I do not cry.

The three of us in the room—the craggy-faced doctor behind the desk, my husband, and I—are quiet for what seems like several minutes. The words, *Be still and know that I am God*, pop into my head right before the doctor's voice slices through the silence, and I jump. He talks about metabolic things and says something that makes me think of sugar. I hear the words "hereditary" and "rare." He clears his throat.

"There are about a hundred known cases worldwide, and well, dammit . . . it's just plain bad luck that the two of you have the same recessive gene. There's no cure at this point. The current treatment is a liver transplant."

He says this like he is reading from an appliance manual, as my throat constricts so that I can hardly breathe. I want him to stop talking. Maybe if I grab him by the throat he'll shut up. See how he likes it, hot fingers clamped around his neck so he can't breathe. I look down and pick at the side of my thumb.

He continues. "My advice? Don't go researching this thing; it'll only scare you half to death. Medical science is always stumbling on some new discovery. Go home, enjoy your son, and hope for a breakthrough.

A breakthrough? A new discovery? You mean miracle! I want to scream. Again, words pop into my head: *Trust Me.*

Really, God? I think. *I'm dangling on the edge of a cliff here.*

My husband is shaking the doctor's hand and ushering me toward the door. Common courtesy, for the moment, trumps grief.

I become a beggar that day—like the roadside paralytic in the Bible who was at the mercy of any passerby with a shred of compassion. Instead of atrophied legs, though, I have withered dreams. No more imagining my son starting school or getting his driver's license. Instead, I dream of his placement on a liver-transplant list. I cry. I scream. I resort to inward pleading and covert bargaining. I make impossible promises: *I'll study the Bible. I'll evangelize my neighborhood. I'll become a missionary.* Like I can twist God's arm. Like He doesn't know what is going on in my life.

He never once speaks a clear word to me about healing. He never promises me anything except one thing: I can trust Him.

The "be still" verse shows up in my thoughts when I least expect it: On a good day when my son is able to stand by himself. On a bad day when I can see the outline of his swollen liver through his belly.

The only words I want to hear are, "We have a match." I am earthbound, tempted by the natural world around me to believe there is nothing else beyond what I can see and comprehend. I want that organ.

WBZ Radio out of Boston becomes my friend, telling me about all the new transplants taking place at Children's Hospital. The stories of another child receiving a new liver draw me in like a lonely old woman seduced by a romantic soap opera. I do a dangerous thing: I form pictures in my mind of each child. I see the color of their hair, the dimples in their hands. I imagine their parents and where they live.

I see their cribs and their toys, and I cheer when their surgeries are a success, hopeful that I, too, will be rejoicing one day. But when one of them doesn't pull through, and most of them don't, fear—ever present in the shadows of my mind—rises up during my sleep and taunts me.

Be still . . .

There is a bigger picture I need to see, and God soon leads me to it.

The radio quiets me. Thoughts of the children and their families calm me. In the daily routine of opening baby food jars, singing lullabies, and listening to the soothing monotone of Dave Maynard on 'BZ reporting the latest details of a transplant patient at Children's Hospital, I slowly become aware of my own selfishness. For my son to live, another child has to die—suddenly would be best, a car accident perhaps, a fall down the stairs, a drowning in a neighbor's pool.

I have never prayed the words, "Dear God, when the surgeon comes to the parents and asks them if he can cut out their baby's liver and place it in my son's body so he can live happily ever after, please make them say yes. Amen." But I may as well have, because it is becoming clear to me that is what needs to happen if God is to answer my prayers for a liver for my child. How can my husband and I be in one part of the hospital rejoicing that our son is going to live, while a few short corridors away, another mom and dad are reeling and shell shocked because now they have to plan a funeral?

. . . and know . . .

Something shifts inside me. I don't know how or when, but I begin thanking God. I thank Him for giving me my son and for ordaining the number of days he will have on Earth. I thank Him for helping me to trust Him for the length of those days and to be grateful for them.

Some days God feels as close as the air I breathe. He comforts me as I lay on a cot in a playroom at Children's Hospital the week before Christmas, the breathing of the other parents who lay there with me slow and soft, all of us sharing a burden in our pretense of sleep. God speaks peace to my heart in the lab as I sing "Jesus Loves Me" into my son's screaming face while he kicks me during his monthly blood test. And when I am expecting my second child, He gives me the confidence to deny the genetic counselor access to my pregnant belly.

It is summer, and the older woman sitting across from my husband and me has a thick Indian accent.

"You realize the chances are the same for each pregnancy that you could have another child with this condition?" she asks.

I blink, then silently look at my husband.

The counselor shuffles some papers. "We'll get you scheduled for an amniocentesis as soon as possible."

"What for?" I ask.

"To determine if the fetus you're carrying has this condition, of course."

"I mean, why would we do that?"

"Well, because . . . so . . . (she clears her throat) . . . you can make a choice."

"I'm not doing that. I mean, we're not having. . . ." I cannot speak the word.

She frowns. She glances at my husband, then looks directly at me. "The chances are one in four the fetus will present this disease, fifty percent it will be a carrier. For—each—pregnancy." She says this like she's grounding me because I didn't clean my room.

"We're not having amnio." My voice is strong, but then spit begins to pool behind my teeth. I think, *Great, I've just put my new baby before the firing squad.*

. . . I am God.

It is late autumn. The air is cold and it smells like winter is right around the corner. My son is approaching his fourth birthday, and the two of us are running through the leaves. I run into the house to check on his baby sister, who is perfect and napping in her blanket, and to grab the camera. When I come back out, my son smiles big for me, the sharp air causes tears to form in his blue eyes. That's when I see it: Life. Pink, chubby, toddler-grinning life looking right at me. We laugh. My son laughs because the sun is bright and the leaves are funny and he is having his picture taken. I laugh because my boy is running. Because his liver is shrinking back to normal and he's been denied placement on the liver-transplant list. Because we are moving to Maine, far away from Children's Hospital and WBZ Radio and doctors who scratch their heads wondering if they are witnessing a miracle. For a brief moment, worry over moving away from family and friends tries to cast a shadow over my smiling heart. But then I hear again: *Trust me.* And I turn it over to God. And I don't turn on the radio all day.

It Is a Gift to Receive

Nancy Tusinski

The first time I attended a foot-washing service on Maundy Thursday was at a Roman Catholic Church in New Hampshire about eleven years ago. Although I wanted to go up and have my feet washed, my stomach churned at the thought of letting someone wash my feet. It made me feel vulnerable and exposed. As I watched others go up, I slipped off one shoe, then the other. As I watched folks walk back to their seats barefoot, I took off my socks. *Okay,* I said to myself, *you can do this.* I got up and walked slowly to the front of the church and sat down on the wooden chair at the end of the row.

In front of me was Bob from the 7:30 early morning service. Bob carefully knelt down on his seventy-two-year-old knees next to the basin of water, placed the towel over his shoulder, ever so gently picked up my foot, and washed it slowly and reverently as though it were the most precious thing on earth. I looked down at Bob's face as he washed my foot, and God's love for me came pouring out of Bob and into me. In that moment, I felt like I finally "got" the other half of Jesus' message. I had understood His message of service and giving, but I'd never really understood His message of receiving God's love.

I'm a New England gal. I don't receive things very well—not compliments, not assistance, not free offers. I was raised to be pretty self-sufficient and to "pull myself up by my bootstraps." If I didn't do it, who would? If someone offered help, I would usually say, "Oh no; that's all right," or "No thanks; I can manage." If someone gave me a gift, I would say, "Oh, you shouldn't have."

I didn't realize until Bob held my foot in his hands that by refusing these offers of help, I was refusing gifts from God. I was refusing to have my feet washed. I was refusing communion. I was refusing love.

As I walked back to my pew, a little picture show rushed into my head of all the times I had refused offers of help or discounted people's good words to me. Now I felt as though with each offer of help, God had been holding out a beautiful present that I turned away from or just knocked right out of His hands. But I also remembered times that I had accepted help.

One year near Thanksgiving, when my children were

little, we had a house fire in the middle of the night and lost everything but the pajamas we were wearing. We were not hurt. I was twenty-four years old, and my husband was twenty six. My daughter was five years old, and my son was seven months old. People we knew and people we didn't know brought clothes, baby food, furniture, toys for the kids, and Christmas decorations. Even though the decorations were plastic, ugly, and worn, they were gorgeous to me. There have been twenty-seven Christmases since the fire, and I hang those decorations on my tree every year. Jesus washed my feet after the fire.

I was a single parent for many years and had very little money. We lived on a small farm in a small town in New Hampshire. Like most small towns, word got out about who was celebrating and who was hurting. One Saturday when I went to the local feed store to pick up grain, Crazy Uncle Billy (the name everyone, including Billy, called himself), who was one of the owners, took me aside and said that he was getting too old and too tired and too cranky to write the monthly newsletter and sale flyer. He asked if I would be willing to take this on—but they couldn't pay me cash; they would have to pay me in grain and hay. I nodded my head. I couldn't speak. Crazy Uncle Billy put out his hand.

"Then it's a deal," he said. I nodded my head again, got in my car, and cried all the way home. Jesus washed my feet at the Rochester Hill feed store.

A few years later, hard times hit again. After being laid off from my job, I had to find a cheaper place to live. I found a little apartment in a rundown neighborhood in South Berwick, Maine. When I looked at the apartment, it was filthy, but the landlady assured me it would be cleaned before I moved in. A few days before the move, on my way to lunch with some friends, I stopped by the apartment and it was still filthy. I called the landlady and she said I'd have to clean it myself; her cleaning person was sick. I looked around and thought, *It will take ten people to clean this apartment.*

I arrived at the restaurant feeling pretty depressed about the whole situation—losing a job I loved, moving from a little house I loved, and now this mess of an apartment to clean. Over lunch, I shared all this with Cindy and Wendy. They immediately offered to help, but I refused. I was embarrassed to have them see where I was going to live, and this really wasn't their problem.

"Please let us help," Cindy said.

"It'll be fun," Wendy said. "We'll bring some music and have a cleaning party!"

That's just what we did. We worked really hard, and we laughed harder. Wendy even brought curtains and some other extra things she "wasn't using." My friends brought hope and joy to my new house, and my feelings about the apartment changed that day. Jesus washed my feet in South Berwick, Maine.

Yet, up until that Maundy Thursday service eleven years ago, I thought these were just random acts of kindness. Just people offering to help. Sometimes, I still mistake them for "just people." But they're not. I now understand that all the strangers who helped us after the fire, Crazy Uncle Billy, Cindy and Wendy, and anyone who comes to me offering help or a good word, they are just like Bob, cradling and washing my foot with tenderness, transmitting God's love through their hands. They come bearing gifts from God. They come bearing His message, "Love one another as I have loved you."

Bless the Weeds and the Children

Diane Stark

It was the best time of my whole day. My children's homework was finished, and they were outside playing. Dinner was in the oven and would be ready in 20 minutes. That meant I had 20 whole minutes to do whatever I chose. Sighing with contentment, I sat down and opened the novel I'd been longing to read. I'd read just two paragraphs when my six-year-old daughter, Julia, burst through the door.

"Mommy, will you go on a walk with me? Yesterday I saw these beautiful yellow flowers, and I want to go and pick some," she said.

"How far is it?" I asked.

"Oh, not far."

I glanced at the oven timer. 17 minutes. So much for a little "me" time. Sighing, I put down my novel and followed Julia outside.

When we reached the sidewalk, she grabbed my hand and swung our clasped hands through the air as we walked. She told me about her day, and I told her about mine. It was nice—for a few minutes.

"Hey, Jules, how much farther is it? Dinner is going to be ready soon, and I need to get back home to take it out of the oven."

"Oh, it's not much farther, Mommy," she said, still swinging my hand.

But five minutes later we were still walking. "Where are these flowers, honey? I really need to get back home," I said.

"Oh, we're getting really close," she assured me with a grin.

A few minutes later, Julia pointed and said, "Look, Mommy, here they are! The flowers I was talking about!"

I looked around, expecting to see some pretty little wild flowers. But all I saw was a field full of dandelions. "Where, Jules? Where are the flowers?"

She pointed again, right at the dandelions. "They're right there, Mommy. Don't you see them?"

"Silly girl, those aren't flowers. They're dandelions. They're actually weeds, remember?"

"Oh, well, I like them. I think they're pretty. Can I pick some?"

I sighed and said, "Yes, but hurry up. I'm sure dinner is done by now."

On the way back, Julia skipped, her hands full of dandelions. I moped along beside her, my hands empty, my head full of negative thoughts. *I could have been reading my book, but instead I walked all over the neighborhood to pick a bunch of weeds. Weeds we already have in our own yard.*

My attitude didn't improve as I ate my dry, over-baked chicken, either. *I ruined our dinner for dandelions,* I thought sourly.

At bedtime, I went into Julia's room to tuck her in. She bowed her head to pray.

"Dear God, thank You for a great day. Thank You for the warm sunshine and for a fun recess at school today. Thank You that Mommy and I had so much fun on our walk, even though the flowers I saw turned out to be just weeds. Thank You for my Mommy, who puts weeds in a vase just to make me happy. Amen."

Julia raised her head, opened her eyes, and smiled at me. "Thank you, Mommy."

I nestled her head under my chin so she wouldn't see my tears. "No, thank you, Jules," I said softly.

And thank You, too, Lord, for the gift of my little girl, the one who helps me to see flowers where others might see weeds. And Lord, help me to remember that life is about the journey and how incredibly blessed I am to have someone like Julia skipping along beside me.

This story was first published in the periodical 909, June 2010.

Caught

JoAnne Potter

I don't know why I just walked in today. I trust them. I really do. I've gone to Rachel's apartment unexpectedly a dozen times. Both David and Rachel specifically asked me to do this as part of their commitment to self-control during their courtship, but today, rather than waiting for one of them to come to the door, I rapped once sharply, pushed inside, turned into the living room calling, "Hi, kids. It's Mom," and stopped midstride. They just looked at me. They didn't even move.

Only twice have I seen David show real fear. The first time, he was almost two and falling down the stairs. Then, I had only to thrust my arms out in time to catch him before he hit bottom, pat him a few times until we both understood he was unhurt, set him back on his little feet, and send him on his way. The second time was today, twenty years later, and he was falling again.

I had no words for this situation. I'd used them all already.

"Go slow, David."

"Love is not a feeling, David. It's a commitment."

"You don't know her yet, David. Give it time."

"Guard your heart. Value your purity and hers."

No, there was nothing to say. I closed my eyes, turned around, and put one heavy foot in front of the other.

"Mom, stop. Mom, please wait." David pushed past to block my way.

"Why, David?"

"Mom, I'm sorry. Please come back. We need to talk."

"We've already talked."

He hung his head. "Mom, we can't do this. No. . . . I can't do this. Dad told me to be strong. I'm trying, but when I get around Rachel, I just lose my head." Something caught in his throat. "Please help."

"I can't. We've already told you what to do. You have already gone too far, and you know it. If you really want to do this right, then you'll walk out with me right now."

All the years of training, all the months of watching to see which way he would go, came to this moment. Flesh pulled me one way, my heart the other. I knew my Lord would not release David from His loving care, but David could choose to run away. I felt the old adrenaline-filled panic reflex and wanted to reach out again to grab him, but couldn't.

Neither of us spoke on the way home. I thought of Jesus' sad prayer for His beloved Jerusalem: "How often I have longed to gather your children together, as a hen gathers her chicks under her wings, but you were not willing."

Would David be willing?

After we pulled into the driveway, I went in but he lingered a long time in the car, shoulders slumped and shuddering. I watched only a moment from the window. I'd comforted the crying boy many times. Today, the man must weep alone.

Eventually, the front door closed behind him and he stood drawn up in the middle of the room, chin steady and shoulders square.

"Mom, you're right. Rachel and I are in way over our heads. Self-control is part of love and we need to learn it. From now on, she and I will not be alone together anywhere. We will do whatever it takes to conduct ourselves righteously before God and win back your trust. If she doesn't agree, well, maybe she isn't the one for me after all."

I looked down to make sure my hands still hung at my

sides. They did. Years ago, I had caught David in mid-air to rescue him from hurt. Today, I could do nothing, but when David fell, he still landed safely. Arms much stronger than mine had caught him this time.

Jesus Took the Wheel

Susan Kelly Skitt

It happened in the blink of an eye one February afternoon. My sons were in school, and I had an important meeting with clients for my new jewelry business. I pulled out of our driveway onto the busy country road. Down the hill I drove, following behind a white car at a safe distance, enjoying the familiar view of majestic trees arching into the blue sky and houses nestled in the woods.

As I rounded the curve, I noticed a car driving up the hill toward me cross the double yellow line. *He's going to correct himself, isn't he?* I thought. *If he doesn't, he'll hit—*"Oh no!" I screamed out loud, my heart hammering in my chest, my thoughts whirling: *He's on my side of the road! He's going to hit the car in front of me! I'm going to drive right into the middle of the accident!*

A split second later, I saw the cars collide and heard the sickening thud of metal, screeching tires, and breaking glass. Yanking my steering wheel hard to the right, I called out "Help me, Lord!" and jammed both feet onto my brake pedal as my car plunged down the sloping embankment. I was heading straight for the large picture window of a stone house, and I couldn't stop. My hands gripped the steering wheel and my anti-lock brakes *thump, thump, thumped* as my car surged closer and closer to the house. "Oh, dear Jesus, I am going to hit this house. I am going to die just like my first husband."

Time seemed to stand still, until at the last moment my large SUV came to an abrupt stop a few feet from the house. I jammed the gear shift into park, then lay my head on the steering wheel. My whole body shook. By God's grace, I was alive—rattled, but okay.

Suddenly, I heard someone crying out. I looked out my car window in the direction of the cries and realized they were coming from the white car that had been struck. I wanted to just leave. I had to get to that meeting for my new business, but the story of the Good Samaritan flashed through my mind. *Susan, if you leave, you'll be just like the priest and the Levite in that story Jesus told in the Bible. You would be leaving a person in need.*

I opened my car door and stumbled up to the road. The elderly woman in the white car moaned. "Help me, oh, someone help me." Other cars had stopped, and two men stood on either side of her vehicle. Her front windshield was shattered, and the driver's side of her car was smashed. My head felt like it was spinning. I wouldn't be much help. What could I do?

"We need to get her out of there," one man yelled. He tried to open the driver's side door, but it wouldn't budge.

The man standing on the passenger side said, "Maybe we should wait for the ambulance."

I agreed. What if she was hurt and we injured her further by moving her?

The first man shook his head. "We've got to get her out of there. The car could explode." He ran around the front of the car and yanked open the passenger door. He reached inside for the elderly woman and gently pulled her out of the car. I immediately grasped her arm so she wouldn't fall. Together, each of us holding one of the elderly driver's arms, we walked her a safe distance away from the car, across the driveway of the stone house to a concrete step.

"I was just driving to drop off my taxes." The woman's voice trembled.

I helped the woman sit down on the step and gently brushed chips of broken glass from her body.

"Are you okay? The ambulance is on its way."

"I think so." The elderly woman touched her head. Shards of glass fell from her hair. Blood dripped from cuts on her face and arms. "Can someone call my son? He works nearby."

I ran to my car a few yards behind me. I had left the door open and the engine running. After grabbing my cell phone and turning off the ignition, I looked at how close my car was to the front of the house. It was as if God had put an angel in front of my car like a miraculous unseen barrier.

I sat down next to the elderly woman. "What's your son's name?"

"Jim."

"That's my husband's name. My name is Susan."

The woman smiled and gripped her purse. "My name is Lois."

"Lois. Wow! Can you believe it? That's my mother-in-law's name too. She lives right up this road next to my house."

"Oh, wait until I tell my son." Her hands shook. "I have another son named Dave."

"You're not going to believe this, but my husband's

brother's name is Dave." I grinned. "My husband also has a sister named Diane."

Lois chuckled. Light danced in her eyes. "I have a daughter, too, but her name is not Diane."

After making a phone call to her son, I sat on the step and gently rubbed the woman's back. She was probably the same age and size as my mother-in-law, mid-seventies and petite. Moments later my cell phone rang.

"Hello?"

"Sue, where are you?" My friend's voice said over the phone. "We're all here waiting."

My friend had set up the lunch meeting to help me get started in my new jewelry business. Three clients waited with her in a restaurant.

"You're not going to believe what happened." I stood up and walked away, quickly explaining the events that had transpired. "I can't leave. I can't make the meeting. Please tell them I'm sorry."

I snapped my cell phone shut. When I returned, Lois was talking to a man standing in front of her. I sat down. When there was a break in the conversation, I spoke.

"Lois, I was in the car right behind you. I saw everything

that happened. The man in the car crossed the line and hit you. It was his fault. When the police get here, I'll tell them everything."

She lifted her hand and pointed to the man in front of her. "This is the man who hit me."

Red hot anger surged through me. How dare he stand here? I swallowed hard. Well, at least he had stopped—unlike the person who had run my first husband off the road and killed him, causing me to become a young widow with a nine-month-old child. Nobody had seen that accident from start to finish. But I saw this one, and I was going to make sure this man would pay.

Lois opened a little notebook and wrote down the man's name.

That's right, Lois, I thought to myself. *Write down that man's name. He's going to be held responsible.*

"I'm going to be praying for you," she said to the man.

I couldn't believe my ears.

Lois turned to me. "This poor man just came from getting a cancer treatment. He hasn't been well." She looked at the man, compassion filling her eyes. "I am going to put you on our church prayer list."

My heart prickled. *This man caused the accident, and she is going to pray for him?*

A small, quiet voice spoke to me in that moment: *Susan, isn't that what you're supposed to do? Isn't that what I've told you to do in my Word?* I thought about all the Bible lessons I had learned through the years at church. I thought about my quiet times reading God's Word and how much God had taught me about His mercy and grace. But today, on the side of a rural Pennsylvania road, I learned a lesson in forgiveness I would never forget.

The police and ambulance soon arrived. Lois's son Jim took care of his mom. After writing my statement, a police officer walked me to my car.

"We have the road blocked off so you can back your vehicle onto the road," he said.

I stared at the flashing lights of the police cars.

"You know," the officer remarked, "when you drove off the road, if you had been only a few feet to your left, you would have hit a telephone pole. A few more feet to the right, the embankment is deep and filled with trees. There's probably no other spot where you would have avoided impact."

I marveled at the path my car had taken off the road, down the embankment, and across the grass and simply nodded. My Lord was in control. He took the wheel and steered me in the right direction—to safety . . . and to forgiveness.

My Journey from Judgment to Love

Toianna Wika

Recently, while sitting in silence before the service began at my church, I felt a kind of despair. I could not stop thinking about the lack of kindness, compassion, and charity that I seemed to see everywhere I looked, worst of all in the religious community affiliated with the school our children attend. The prevailing attitude within this particular religious community had even led me to question my Catholic faith.

I was particularly distressed by the disrespect and intolerance that many in the school had expressed toward other Christian sects. Their declarations that Christian marriages outside of the Catholic Church are invalid and their denial of communion to other Christians on the grounds that they do not really understand the Word of God like Catholics do did not fit with my Christian values.

Now, sitting in my own church, I remembered the many instances of hurtful gossip, judgments, and apathy I had witnessed in my children's school. Rather than the devout group of Christians I had sought, this religious community seemed to be a self-righteous posse.

The harder I tried to think through my dilemma, the more upset I became. So I gave my problem to God and began flipping through our church bulletin, where I discovered many quotes by Mother Teresa, in honor of what would have been her one-hundredth birthday.

The first quote to leap off the page was this:

"There is only one God to all. Therefore, it is important that everyone is seen as equal before God. I've always said we should help a Hindu become a better Hindu, a Muslim become a better Muslim, a Catholic become a better Catholic . . ."

The next Mother Teresa quote to strike a chord was: "There are so many religions, and each one has its different ways of following God. I follow Christ. Jesus is my God . . . Jesus is my Everything."

Mother Teresa's words were validation enough for me that my views are not heresy.

But God had yet another message for me that Sunday. The scriptural reading concerned Luke 13:23–24 (NKJV): ". . . Strive to enter in through the narrow gate, for many, I say to you, will attempt to enter but will not be able."

Our rector talked about how the criteria to enter

Heaven will be having loved God and others. As Father Johnson spoke, I thought about how conservative a Catholic he is, yet he had allowed those words of Mother Teresa to be published in our parish bulletin. In fact, he had probably selected them. The only way I could explain his having included the quotes was that he was on a similar path as Mother Teresa.

I realized that, although Father Johnson was firm in his doctrinal convictions and his love for God, he constantly demonstrated that he was equally firm in his resolve to have an open heart to others. He was actually practicing what I had decided long ago is the crux of all God's laws— that we love Him foremost and then our neighbors as ourselves (Matthew 22: 36–40).

As I compared my own attitudes and actions regarding the school community with those of Mother Teresa and Father Johnson, I realized that while my motives for questioning them had originated from love, most of my actual words and actions were judgmental. And they were not loving. A quote by Saint Teresa of Avila that I had wrestled with since college came to mind, and this time it made sense: "The road to Hell is paved with good intentions."

For years, I had spouted loudly about how Christians have it backward, with their generous handing out of judgment but tendency to leave the loving to God, rather than following what God instructs in Matthew 22: 36–40. I tried to visualize how it would look for me to love without judgment. To my surprise, I could not. I was forced to face that I had become one of the most judgmental individuals I knew. That realization brought to mind another quote from Mother Teresa: "If you judge people, you have no time to love them."

In truth, the only thing I had done right so far about my problem with the religious school community was to return to our home parish week after week for perspective, to hear enough of what I needed to keep me going. Even then, I had stopped going to church for a couple of months while I questioned whether to leave the Catholic church altogether, despite my clear calling to join several decades ago.

Not only had my focus become one of judgment rather than love, it had also contributed to my own struggle with negativity. I had been exuding anger, hurt, paranoia, and defensiveness toward the school community, which had attracted similar emotions and reactions from them, which had only generated more of those ugly feelings on my part. Despite having known that whatever I put out will come back and expand in my own life, I had somehow lost track of that fact and created the emotional tornado that was devouring my ability to show kindness, compassion, and charity myself.

What would happen, I wondered, if, rather than pointing a finger, I helped to create positive experiences for others in the school and church community? What would happen if I visited with a smile on my face and an attitude of humility, service, and love in my heart?

I had taken the first step. I had been open and receptive to seeing how the problem was mostly an inside job. I realized that to build on my revelation, I needed to humble myself and empty myself of all the toxic judgment in confession, then work and pray my way back into a focus of love, rather than judgment.

Once I was able to get past the humiliation of my own hypocrisy, I felt renewed and peaceful, full of expectation and child-like excitement about the adventure sure to follow. I prayed silently that God would help me to embrace Francis of Assisi's prayer, "Make Me a Channel of Your Peace."

Long after Mass ended that day, the words of Mother Teresa echoed in my head and in my heart: "I am a little pencil in the hand of a writing God who is sending a love letter to the world."

Twice Blessed

Kathryn Lay

When the doctor told me I was pregnant, I couldn't believe it had finally happened.

A month later, when he told me I wasn't, I didn't want to believe it.

For seven years my husband and I had prayed and hoped and dreamed about the day we would learn we were expecting a baby. We talked about how we would tell everyone and begin preparing the nursery right away.

And so we did. After I told the doctor my symptoms and he'd done a quick examination, he confirmed my suspicions. Grinning, I practically floated into the waiting room to tell my husband. We spent the day going from parent to parent and friend to friend sharing our joy.

It was especially exciting to deliver the great news to our best friends from college, who were expecting their first child in a few weeks. Tammy and I had shared so much through college, dating, and our marriages. It was hard to admit that I had been jealous, that it hurt every time we talked about her pregnancy or I saw her. It had been hard to fight back the tears at her baby shower, which I had hosted. Now, I rejoiced that I would be able to truly share the experience of pregnancy and parenting with Tammy.

Anxious to set up our nursery, Richard and I began by replacing the old carpet. We started shopping at garage sales and visiting baby stores to drool over the things we hoped to put in our baby's room.

Over the next few weeks, I spoke often with Tammy. By now a pregnancy expert in her eighth month, she told me about what to expect as my pregnancy progressed.

Then, at my next prenatal checkup, the doctor could not detect a heartbeat at what should have been the end of my first trimester. So he ran further tests.

I sat in the room, my heart pounding. Had I lost the baby and not realized it? I prayed for my baby, for myself, for a miracle.

When the doctor returned, he scratched his head and told me that I had never been pregnant. His partner, the doctor who had told me I was pregnant a month before, had done only a quick pregnancy test and exam. This doctor, having been unable to detect a heartbeat, did a blood test, an exam, and a sonogram. The test results told the true tale: It had all been in my mind. My heart had wanted to conceive a child so badly that my body had followed along with the dream. It was a false pregnancy . . . and the death of my dream.

I sat in the car, numb, unable to make a decision about what to do next. I couldn't contact my husband at work. I didn't feel like telling my mom yet. Suddenly, I knew who to talk with. I knew where I could find the emotional help I needed.

Crying all the way to Tammy's house, I knocked on her door and heard a baby cry. She invited me in, holding her week-old son.

She was as shocked at the news as I was, and she spent the afternoon comforting me. Even in the midst of her joy, she was able to share my hurt and pain. I know she must have had things she wanted to tell me about, new faces or movements little Jonathan made. But she let me do the talking that afternoon. I cried for the Michael or Michelle I had imagined.

God had put this special friend in my life. For many years, we had been two best friends sharing life's ups and downs. We were sisters in our heart and through our faith in God.

Six years later, Tammy was there when Richard and I spent months filling out paperwork and attending classes to become adoptive parents. She was there when we were approved. She was there to celebrate the night we received the call that we had a baby—a daughter whose birth name was Michelle, just as I would have given her. Tammy was there to meet our daughter the first day we took her home to join our family.

As I watch Tammy's three children and my daughter grow, I remember how she held my hand, listened to my sadness, and let me cry when I lost the Michelle of my dreams. I remember how she held my hand, listened to my joy, and let me cry tears of happiness when I found the Michelle of my heart.

God blesses women with so much, but when we are blessed with the love of another woman's friendship, it is easy to see how much God truly loves us.

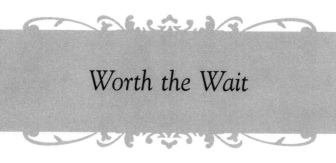

Worth the Wait

Taryn R. Hutchison

"There's this great guy . . ." my well-meaning friends, Frank and Cora, told me.

I'd heard that one before.

"Thanks, but no," I said. "Just can't handle anything long-distance right now. I mean, I'm trying my best to adjust to life in Florida. California's too far away."

I didn't give Frank and Cora a chance to tell me the lucky guy's name. If I had, I could've told them that not only did I know him, but I was having lunch with him the next day.

Still, romance was not on my agenda. My life had been turned upside down, and I was struggling to hold on. After living abroad for ten years, I'd recently returned to the States. The transition back home seemed every bit as daunting as when I'd left. Life in the U.S. had changed during my decade away, but I had changed more.

Besides, I'd given up on the idea of getting married. I'd turned forty while hidden away as a missionary in Eastern

Europe. Eligible men had been something of a rarity. I'd been so caught up in my ministry that I hadn't noticed my clock run out on the possibility of motherhood.

Don't get me wrong. It's not that I didn't want to get married and have children and live happily ever after. I grew up believing in fairy tales and playing house, like most girls did. I never stopped believing in the deepest part of my heart that God could still do the impossible in my life, even at my age and in that remote place in the world. But until and unless He chose to bring the right guy along, I didn't need a husband; I merely wanted one. My completeness was in Christ alone, and I could trust Him to provide everything I needed.

My hope had been deferred for so long that I'd laid it to rest. I no longer asked God for what I wanted. I stopped hoping. And I grieved the loss of what might have been.

When I felt especially tired or lonely overseas, weak hopes resurfaced. Holidays spent alone, when something beautiful made me ache to share it with someone special that was when I'd remember the good ones I'd let go—like Steve—and imagine what life would be like if I hadn't.

Steve and I met when I was in my twenties. I saw him from a distance that day in church. How could I not notice him? I had never seen such a handsome guy before. Tall and dark, he had a captivating smile. Steve asked for my phone number that day and called me as soon as I got home. I had never experienced that kind of self-confidence in guys.

During our first date, Steve got straight to the point. He told me he wasn't interested in casual dating; he wanted a serious relationship with me. His kind heart and positive spirit attracted me, but I feared rebound when he said he was recently divorced with two small kids. Besides, I already sensed God calling me to Eastern Europe. Steve and I were clearly headed in opposite directions. Not wanting to string him along needlessly, I broke up with Steve before it began. I told him I wanted to be friends but we did not have a romantic future together.

When I felt especially lonely overseas, I wondered if I'd made the right decision.

Now I was back in California, visiting with friends like Frank and Cora. Steve was one of those friends. I hadn't seen him in ten years, and it had been fourteen years since our one and only date.

"Hi! Do you remember me?" I asked him over the phone.

"Do I remember you?" he said. "Taryn, you are unforgettable."

We arranged to meet for lunch the next day. Our date on that warm July day stretched into the evening. We talked about everything. The time flew by, and we never ran out of things to say. When Steve guided me into the restaurant with his hand on the small of my back, I felt butterflies from his touch. Later that evening, we said goodbye at my car. I would leave California the next day. I didn't know when, or if, I'd see him again. Unlike our first date so many years before, this time Steve kept his cards close to his chest.

As I drove away, I thought that Steve shouldn't be alone. I prayed as I drove, asking God to give him a wife to love him. My prayers are not always so selfless, but this time I thought about Steve, not about me.

In the quiet places in my heart, I sensed the Lord communicating with my spirit: *I am giving him a wife—you.* The thought thrilled me. Still, I didn't know if Steve had received this same nudging.

When I returned to my desk in Florida, five e-mail messages from Steve waited for me in my in-box. That's when I knew. My long-dormant hope was resuscitated.

Our coast-to-coast courtship sped by. We already knew each other well, and we had been carrying a flame for each other for fourteen years. We had no reason to prolong things. We talked a lot on the phone, e-mailed daily, and handwrote long letters to each other. Steve visited me once in Florida, and I flew to California to see him at Christmastime. He created feasts that we ate in front of a crackling fire and took me for walks in the hills. We sat on the patio in the evenings and listened to crickets chirping. My heart had known he was the man for me since that magical day in July, but I needed to let my mind catch up. We discussed the few remaining issues to be certain.

On the day of the winter solstice, the darkest day of the year but one of the brightest of my life, Steve slipped down onto one knee and asked me to marry him. I didn't hesitate to answer, "Yes!"

Eagerly, we shared our good news with family and friends. Steve called friends who'd been praying for him for years, named Frank and Cora.

"The Frank and Cora from Hillside?" I asked.

Steve nodded.

"I know them. Did you happen to mention who you're engaged to?"

"Nope. Just said I'd bring over my fiancée tomorrow to meet them."

"Hey, let's have some fun with this."

We concocted our surprise. The next day, Steve knocked on Frank and Cora's door and delivered the sad news that his fiancée couldn't make it, while I walked a few laps around the block.

After a sufficient pause, I stood on their doorstep.

"Hi, Frank! I was in the neighborhood . . ." I said.

"Have you ever met our friend, Steve?" he asked.

I thought I detected a twinkle in Cora's eye.

"Why, yes, I think I remember you." I thrust my hand out to Steve. "Good to see you again."

Steve shook my hand vigorously. "That's a beautiful diamond. Anyone I know?"

"Okay, just stop. Stop it right now," Cora said, putting her hands on top of ours. "We know. She's engaged to you, Steve. Come here, you two, and look at something."

We followed her into the kitchen. Today's page in the daily calendar bore the words, "Steve and Taryn stop by."

"How'd you guess?" I asked.

They'd had us in mind for each other all along. After I'd nixed their matchmaking scheme, they decided to stop interfering and to start praying that God would bring us together in His timing. They fully expected He would do just that.

I'd quit praying, but thankfully they hadn't.

Three months later, Steve and I were married.

We try not to take our love for granted. Both of us having been single for so many years, we knew the real fear of never having someone to love. We had waited a long time for the right one, convinced that being alone was much better than settling. Waiting turned out to be a good thing for us. It made us more grateful. And it couldn't thwart God's purpose in our lives.

Sure, there are moments when we wonder, *What if we'd gotten married younger?* I could've helped Steve raise his children. Maybe we would've had kids of our own together. But I might have resented not being able to fulfill my dream of moving to Eastern Europe. I can't imagine my life with that chapter unwritten.

When I told my Eastern European friends the news of my impending marriage, each echoed the same sentiment. "If you had married Steve in the beginning, I never would have met you. I'm glad you waited."

God's timing was perfect. It was worth the wait.

Shirley, Goodness, and Mercy

Judy Gerlach

I lay my sleepy infant down in her crib, wind up the musical mobile with its colorful, whimsical animals dangling above her head, and stroke her soft strawberry-blond hair. Together, Lori and I listen to "Brahms' Lullaby" until her eyes surrender and she falls asleep. It is in moments like this that I stand in awe of God's goodness, wondering how my heart can possibly contain all the love I have for my children without bursting. It is a perfect moment . . . almost.

A recurring pain in my legs reminds me that something is wrong. I have no idea what it is. I know I should seek medical help, but we're new in town and I have yet to find a primary care physician for myself. The possibilities frighten me. I lean on the rail of the crib and wait for the pain to subside. *Please, God,* I silently pray, *make this go away. Help me.* Feeling very much alone in a town full of strangers, I question whether God even hears me.

No time to worry about that right now, though. With my husband, Greg, at work, I must tend to my responsibilities at home. I hobble to a chair in the family room and watch my four-year-old daughter, Lindy, play with a friend while I wait for my nine-year-old daughter, Lisa, to come home from school.

"I hope your legs get better, Mommy," Lindy says, reminding me through a still, small voice that God is near.

I smile at her. Eventually, the pain goes away, and I forget about it.

Life is unpredictable for the next few weeks. During the intervals when I'm able to walk without pain, I manage to catch up with the housework and to do the grocery shopping, leaving our three girls at home with their daddy.

I'm thrilled when Sunday comes and I'm feeling well enough to take the girls to the church we'd visited several times before. The people in the Sunday school class that I attend welcome me with smiling faces. Basking in the warmth of the fellowship, I experience the love of Jesus firsthand. Several friendly ladies introduce themselves to me, but one particular face lingers in my thoughts long after I'm back home. I can't remember her name, but I look forward to seeing her again the next Sunday.

Days pass, and the leg problem comes and goes regularly. My tendency to view life through rose-colored glasses keeps anxiety at bay. But when my faith is put to the test, I find it increasingly difficult to stay strong.

At the end of the week, without warning, I wake up in the middle of the night with a high fever. My knees swell like melons, and the pain becomes excruciating. Strangely, the fever disappears almost as quickly as it came, but I'm unable to walk. My two older girls, mature beyond their years, help me with their baby sister as much as they can.

The next day, the storm clouds burst over us like Niagara Falls. The doctor looks at me and in a very matter-of-fact tone says, "You need to be admitted to the hospital." His voice is calm, but that usually doesn't help when the patient is scared out of her wits to begin with. "How soon can you get over there?"

My emotions run the gamut, all in an instant. A lengthy hospital stay looms on the horizon. We need help, but we hardly know anyone. Greg can't stay home from his new job, and we're not in any position to hire someone. This can't be happening. What about my little girls? My baby? I can't leave my family. This whole thing is out of the question.

My husband manages to keep a level head. "Are there any other options?" he asks.

The doctor's answer is a definitive "no."

Greg tells him we need a few hours to take care of some little details.

Little details? This is huge!

"What do you have in mind to do?" I ask him. "What about your new job? Who's going to watch our kids?" I shake my head. "This won't work."

"Call the church."

"But we don't know anyone there," I argue.

"We don't know anyone else around here, do we?" he counters. "Whatever's wrong with you is getting worse instead of better. We don't have a choice. We have to rely on strangers to help us, one way or the other."

He's right. Everyone in town is pretty much a stranger. Images of all the smiling faces from that Sunday school class float across my mind. But they are faces with no names. Still, I call the church.

The caring voice on the other end of the line reveals genuine concern for my desperate situation. She tells me she'll make a few phone calls, check with some folks who are in the Sunday school class I'd visited, and get back to me. Within the hour, my phone rings.

"I've found someone to keep your girls while you're in

the hospital," the secretary says, "and she doesn't expect any payment."

"The baby, too?" I ask, incredulous that anyone would be willing to take in a four-month-old.

"Yes, ma'am. She and her husband have three children, and their youngest daughter is the same age as your oldest." Her words are sweet music. "They're very nice people, and she says she remembers you from the class. She wants you to call her so you can discuss the details."

She remembers me? In God's amazing Providence, the benevolent soul who has graciously offered to keep my children is Shirley, the same lady whose face I remember so clearly. When I speak with her on the phone, her compassionate voice quickly disarms my overly protective, maternal instincts. I feel as though I'm talking with an old friend. She says she'll come to pick up the girls after school and that my husband can take the rest of their belongings to her house later that day.

From the moment Shirley walks into my bedroom, I feel bowled over by so much love that I almost forget she is still basically a stranger. She's obviously a natural with babies. I watch with intense scrutiny as she picks up my infant daughter and loves on her as if Lori is her own. Still, when the moment comes to release my little girls into the hands of a woman I barely know, that powerful tug at my maternal heartstrings somehow overshadows the fierce pain in my swollen knees. Tears pool in my eyes, and pretty soon my girls dive in with me. But Shirley keeps her cool and finds all the right words—things I want to express but don't know how.

Shirley tells me the church will pray for me. She also tells me that she has made plans for the ladies of the class to bring meals to my family for as long as we need. I want to know how much all that is going to cost.

She looks surprised. "Nothing," she assures me with a smile. "This is what we do when someone needs help."

As I watch her leave with my most precious possessions, I say a little prayer for them as best I can under the circumstances. I know I like Shirley. She must have been heaven sent.

After I'm admitted to the hospital and after surviving a battery of tests for several days, I'm told I have a blood clot behind my left knee. That means staying in the hospital at least another ten days. I also have rheumatic fever. Lonely and depressed, I wait out each day for Greg's report about our girls.

"They miss their mommy, but they're fine," he says. "They're being well taken care of." And he lets me know that the home-cooked meals provided by the ladies from the class are delicious.

That's all I need to know to make it through until I'm well enough to go home. As I heal, I count the days as well as my blessings, so thankful for Shirley and for God's incredible goodness and mercy.

The Only Thing That Matters

Patricia Fish

After spending some quiet morning time praying to my Lord, I reminisce that I am now at the early twilight of my life and marvel at the long, bumpy road to a final, solid landing as a Catholic, the faith into which I was born.

Although it is not about Catholicism, I mentally argue with my Lord, Who answers to all faiths. My Catholicism is as much about my Christianity now as my atheism had been when I was my daughter's age, and my atheism had been as much about my faith as it has been about my total failure to raise my daughter in any religious faith whatsoever.

It all becomes a tangled mental morass as I make my ending sign of the cross and smile to my Lord over how it all turned out.

I was cool. I was so cool that anyone standing next to me risked frostbite from the coolness of my young self who knew it all. And I knew there was no God; only fools believed such nonsense.

When my philosophy college professor assigned an essay in which we would expand on our religious faith and how it all came about, I knew, what with my coolness and hipness and college-level intellect, that it was time to proclaim, in writing, the Truth as I then solidly knew it.

"Why I Am an Atheist" was the title of that incredibly cool, hip, and happening essay. In the narrative I handily listed the many reasons why I knew God didn't exist, why the masses are all fooled into believing God does exist so that we might behave, why I no longer was fooled, and why I was so cool, so hip, and oh so smart. The professor loved the thing and gave me an A+. That cemented the deal, but of course. I was so cool, so hip, so in tune with the "divine" truth that even my betters were touched by my coolness.

All of this could have been just a blip in the timeline of my life, except that, well, I really believed it! I had cast off the heavy garments of my born faith. The Catholic church was oppressive, prone to a grandiose display that I found off-putting during that long-haired, scruffy, hippie era. Pouring waters on babies, singing tomes in Latin, eating stuff and calling it God . . . it was all too heavy and pompous. I threw it all off of me like a damning scourge.

Within two years of this epiphany of coolness, I had

my first child. Still, I was cool. Bringing forth new life does bestow a certain gravity to one's life, however, so I thus became a bit less anti-God. But I remained anti-organized religion, Catholicism being at the top of that list.

"I will not baptize her or otherwise confine her to any religion," I told my husband with firmness of purpose. "We will allow her to grow and develop and choose her own faith. I will not prejudice her with my own agnosticism, but neither will I burden her with adherence to an oppressive faith just because it was my childhood faith."

Indeed, the new term for my fuzzy faith became "agnostic," which is really an atheist with caveats, just in case there might really be a God. However nobly I phrased it, the de facto result of this really bad choice was that I denied my innocent newborn the chance to become part of a Christian faith, which she might, much like her mother, shrug off for a lackluster belief at some later time.

I was cool, the coolest parent on the planet.

It happens to us all, every one of us, no matter our faith, no matter our creed, no matter the church we attend. At some point we need our God. At some point we fall upon our knees and pray as if we were a priest, a bishop, a deacon, a pope. In my case it was the loss of my mother—which brought with it some realizations: That there is more, that there is a God. That I'd been blessed with a wonderful mother, that I'd been blessed to live in a wonderful country with a perfect child. That it was time for me to pray to my Lord, to Jesus who died for our sins, to He Who was mightier than me.

My daughter grew up to be a fine child, but she had no religious upbringing. Amazingly, she considered herself to be Christian, but there was no church on Sundays and no need for it. I returned to my Catholic church, but again, it didn't matter, not to my daughter. I desperately wanted her to join me. She refused. Why wouldn't she? At that adolescent era of her life, church was but a pain, an interruption to late Sunday sleep after hip Saturday parties.

In due course, my daughter married—in a courthouse. She had a child, a wonderful and perfect granddaughter who lit up my world. The baby was not baptized, although I pleaded to take her to my church's Catholic font. Again, neither the faith nor the sect of the baptismal font mattered to me. I just didn't want my daughter to make the same mistake I had.

"We're all getting baptized!" my daughter exclaimed breathlessly over the cellular phone waves.

My eyes filled with tears. This happy news came when my granddaughter was fully five years old.

My daughter told me that she, her husband, and my granddaughter had been attending a local church, newly formed and warmly receiving of this new family in the neighborhood. It wasn't, of course, a Catholic church, but again, it didn't matter. While I might have hoped for my daughter's family to join me for Sunday Mass, it was enough that my granddaughter would be raised within the confines of a warm Christian faith and that her parents would be guided by weekly religious services and the fellowship of other Christians.

Today, my granddaughter, at seven, still goes to mass with me during visits. But she is solidly aligned with her parents and the new church they have joined, where all three were baptized one sunny summer morn.

My, *how it all turned out*, I think and smile at the heavens.

I thank my Lord and Savior and say "Amen," knowing that no matter the worship place here on Earth, we would all be in heaven together when my Lord called us all home. We are all Christians, and that is all that matters.

Roller Coaster of Faith

Sally Clark

"All right, Lord. That's it. You've wrung me dry. I give up. You win."

Kneeling next to the bathtub, tears falling onto the carpeted floor, the tub's cold marble on my face felt like an answer from God. "You want me to be miserable, I'll be miserable. I can do that. No problem."

I raised my head and wiped my eyes. I was done. I was resigned. This may not have been what God wanted to hear, but it was all He was getting from me that day. The roller coaster ride was finally over. I was getting off here, and here is where I would stay.

Two years earlier, my husband and I had sold our house in the suburb of a large city and moved 300 miles away to a house in the country, just outside of a small town. We were following our dreams, but six months into our adventure, my husband's employer offered him a better job back in the city, and he decided to take it—without consulting me or God.

My husband complained, "We've been here six months, and you haven't even found us a house to buy yet. I thought you'd be glad to go back to the city where your parents and your friends are."

Maybe he was right. Maybe I was fooling myself that moving to the country was what I had wanted. I couldn't deny I missed the familiarity of our suburban home. I prayed frantically that moving back to the city was the right thing for us to do. But then, I had prayed that moving to the country was the right thing for us, and now we were leaving, and I prayed that I could forgive my husband for not discussing this decision with me.

Back in the city, we ignored our budget and bought a house that was more than we could afford. It didn't take long to realize that we were going to have to withdraw from our savings every month just to make our house payment. Our funds were not unlimited. Sooner than we knew, the money would be gone.

One tearful evening, I confronted my husband with our economic situation. "We have to sell this house and buy something cheaper," I told him.

"No," he replied.

"What do you mean, 'no'?" I said. "Didn't you hear me?

We can't afford this house. Besides, I'm miserable here. I don't like it, and our son is starting to get into real trouble at school. Have you seen those kids he's hanging out with?" I cried.

"No," he said again. "We moved away and now we've moved back, and I'm not moving again. No."

He wouldn't budge. Since I had lost the battle with my husband, I decided to battle with God.

"You've got to help me, Lord. You've got to help us," I pleaded. "Please, Father, don't abandon us here. I hate this. Everything's wrong here. My husband works all the time, and when he's home, all we do is fight. The kids are unhappy. Our son is going to have a criminal record before he's even fourteen years old. Please, Lord, save us. Get us out of this situation before it's too late."

My monologue with God went on for more than a year. I prayed, and cried, everywhere: by the side of my bed, in the bathroom, in the laundry room, at church, at work, in the car. Finally, I decided to give up and submit to His will, whatever that might be. Obviously, it seemed to me, God wanted me to be unhappy. Apparently, I thought, He wanted us to deplete our savings, too. Clearly, I feared, He was prepared to watch our family fall apart and our marriage end. It was that bad.

So I gave up. So did my husband. We would survive as long as we could in this silent stalemate between each other and between ourselves and God, not moving either way. Our faith and our marriage were vanishing right along with our savings.

But when I gave up, everything changed.

On a weekend visit to relatives in the small town we had left behind, one of my cousins mentioned that she planned to buy a building downtown and rent out one side. It was my husband's idea for me to open a small business there. He volunteered to talk to his employer about working in a nearby larger city until I got on my feet.

We put an ad in the newspaper to sell our house. It sold to the first person who looked at it, with a profit that put all the money we'd taken out of our savings account over the previous eighteen months back into it. Within two months of my tearful resignation to the God whose compassion never failed me, we moved back to the small town we loved. Two months later, while driving through a neighborhood of wide, shady streets, my husband spotted a house I had seen almost two years earlier.

"Now, I really like that house," he said.

"Really? I've been in that house. It was on the market when we were here before. It's nice, but it needs a lot of work inside. With the price they're asking, we couldn't afford to do any remodeling. But if you want to see it, I'll call," I said.

After offering the owners 35 percent less than what they were asking, to our surprise, they accepted. We moved in one month later with enough money to completely restore our beautiful old Victorian home. Even better, with eighteen months of counseling, a Christian therapist helped my husband and I rediscover our love for one another.

Now, more than twenty years later, the house we bought has become our home. The small town we adopted long ago adopted us. We opened a business that flourished and enabled us to retire much earlier than we'd planned. Our children grew up, married, and are raising their children here.

Had God been waiting until we gave up to answer our prayers? Did we have to suffer those awful months of pain, worry, and grief in order to learn something about God we might never have known otherwise?

God has blessed us with wonderful joys and comforted us in desperate tragedies, but through it all, we have learned that He is always there—in the joys, in the mourning, and in the silence. He never leaves us. He is always with us. As it is written in Deuteronomy 31:8 (NIV): "The LORD himself goes before you and will be with you; he will never leave you or forsake you."

Released

Katrina Norfleet

Should he slice the cake and take a bite? Or should he save the cake for later? How could he still be trying to figure out how to do both?

Standing in the center of my childhood bedroom with my cell phone to my ear, those were the questions I needed my husband of twelve years to answer. Instead, he made an ill attempt to convince me that after three years of repeatedly going and coming back, he suddenly had clarity and knew what he wanted. If he had been the one listening rather than the one speaking, he might have been able to receive the message as clearly as I did: "I want to be single again, but I don't want to lose my wife and kids."

Maybe I was tired. I had just gotten in from a four-and-a-half-hour drive in a minivan with my mom, my sister, and our three middle-school-age children in tow. Or maybe I was simply worn out from grabbing for the hope that my husband kept dangling just within my reach, then snatched back right when I was about to take hold of it. Maybe it was a combination of both that made the tears flow.

I caught my reflection in the mirror and realized I could as easily have been standing in my bedroom twenty-five years earlier, twisting the long beige cord of the shared house phone between my fingers while crying through a conversation with my teenage sweetheart. But I was a forty-something-year-old woman who was a month shy of commemorating twelve years of marriage with my only husband, father to our two children, second income for our household, co-signer on our mortgage and title to our home, dance partner . . . life partner. For better or worse, we had built what I believed was supposed to stay intact.

It had been more than a year since I'd dropped off my husband at work, kissed him goodbye, and waited for him to return that evening. He never did. Instead, he called and said, "I'm not coming home. I'm not happy." Turns out, he wanted to be separated but not divorced. That would mark our third separation within a two-year span.

I had taken a stand for my marriage all those years because I knew God had instructed me to. I prayed for and believed in the restoration of our marriage. I purchased book after book on the subject, and I found comfort and encouragement in receiving daily devotionals on the subject via e-mail. We tried counseling—first with a male therapist, then with our pastor, then with a female therapist. We even joined the couples ministry at church.

But as I stood in my childhood bedroom, preparing for what was supposed to be a fun-filled family vacation with my mobile flip-phone pressed against my ear, I heard three short words: *You are worthy.*

The voice did not sound like my husband's, nor was it coming through the phone ear piece. Its tone was soft but clear, and it seemed to come from inside of me.

Did I really just hear what I think I heard? I waited, hoping for another message or to at least have those three words whispered to me again. But the only sound was the apologetic drone of the person on the other end of the phone: my estranged husband.

After we finally hung up, I sat on the twin bed, so like the one I had slept on as a child. My eleven-year-old daughter came in and sat down beside me. She could see the tears still pooled inside my eyelids.

"What's wrong?" she asked.

Without taking a moment to censor my answer, I replied with honest emotion. "I'm so mad at your dad because he still doesn't know what he wants to do. One day he says he's coming back, and the next day he changes his mind. I'm even madder that my vacation is going to be ruined now because I'll be thinking about it."

"Well, just don't think about it," she said matter-of-factly before bouncing off the bed and exiting the room.

I loved her childlike response. As if it could be that easy.

But it was. Somehow, I made it through the week without giving much thought to the phone call. Over the next several days, my sister and I replayed our childhood, taking our children to the places we had frequented as kids. It became known as "one of the best vacations ever."

Looking back on that day, it was as if God Himself had whispered the words, "You are worthy," and then reached in and turned a knob, cutting off that emotional desire that kept me wanting to stay bound instead of free. God had reminded me of my value in His sight. I was released from the struggle of holding onto a husband who no longer wanted to be held and from a marriage that had died a slow, painful death. It was like God had also released me from the feeling that I deserved so little, that I was not valuable enough, smart enough, funny enough, thin enough, pretty enough . . . not enough.

Release. Acceptance. Peace. All three came to me, in

that order. It would be the first, the biggest, the hardest, and the most treasured thing I would learn to release to the Master's hand over the next several years.

Five summers have passed since the day I stood in that bedroom talking to my estranged husband on the phone. Over the course of those years, we have gone through court battling, house selling, assets splitting, name calling, finger pointing, and an entire year with no communicating of any sort. Today, we are divorced but friends again, together celebrating our daughter's sweet sixteen and preparing to drive our eldest to college for the first time. I couldn't have imagined this day when I was holding on so tightly to what I wanted instead of what God wanted for me. I thought we were a broken family, but I can see now that with God as the craftsman, anything broken can be made beautiful again, even if it looks different.

Did You Say Angels?

AnneRené Capp

I was just falling asleep, reaching that elusive dreamland of contentment, when I heard a faint voice: "Crystal, you need to wake up."

Refusing to open my eyes, I groggily whined, "Not now, I'm so tired, I need to sleep."

Again, more insistently: "Crystal, it's time for you to wake up and get out of bed."

"I can't, I'm too exhausted."

Continuing to ignore the persistent pleadings, I pulled my quilt up around my neck, rolled over, and burrowed myself deeper into my haven of warmth.

A third beckoning, clear as a bell: "It's time for you to wake up, get out of bed, and come with us."

Finally annoyed, I flung off my covers and begrudgingly sat up on the edge of my bed. "What! What is it that can't wait?"

There was no answer, only a gentle grasp upon each of my elbows as the two beings lifted me to a standing position. Without concern, I was aware that my speaking interactions with these beings were actually thoughts conveyed in a completeness that the spoken word is incapable of expressing. As for the appearance of these beings, I am unable to describe them with shapes and colors or as male and female, for my eyesight was of a spiritual nature. I simply knew they were in my presence and I in theirs, and it felt completely natural.

Gliding slowly, barely above the floor, we entered the living room where they gently set me down in front of our picture window. Not seeing anything unusual, I became irritated and turned toward the two beings.

"What is it you want me to see?" I thought/asked. "There's nothing here!"

"Look outside, behind the drapes."

Conscious that I had not yet actually opened my eyes until this point, I resentfully lifted the edge of the drapes and peered outside. Flames were engulfing our front porch. As I turned around to call out to my family, I realized the beings were gone.

"Fire! Our house is on fire! Paul, Megan, wake up!"

Racing into the living room together, Paul took control. "Megan, go to our designated safety spot in the back yard, and Crystal, call 911, while I get the hose and try to put out the flames."

Once the fire was out, the fire chief approached us.

"Although you have minimal damage to your home, you were incredibly lucky. The smoke from the flames had reached your attic. Normally when that happens, most families sleep right through the fire, because the smoke incapacitates them before the flames ever reach them."

Holding our smoke alarm in his hand, he continued, "We also noticed that your smoke alarm didn't go off."

Interjecting, I said, "I just put a new battery in it last week and tested it, and it worked."

He pushed the manual button on the alarm, and sure enough, it worked . . . then.

"Unbelievable. I don't know what else to say, except that you were lucky all the way around," he said. "I'm curious: were you awake at the time you discovered the fire?"

"No, actually, all of us had been in bed for several hours."

Now looking at me inquisitively, Paul finished, "It was my wife who got us all up."

"What made you get up when you did?" the chief asked me.

"Honestly, I was physically awakened by angels from God."

"Humph. . . . Well, whatever it was, I'm glad you folks are alright," he said as he left.

"Go ahead, Paul," I said. "You and Megan go back to bed. I need some quiet time with the Lord."

Turning off the lights so that I could absorb the beauty of the moonlight filtering into our living room, I settled myself onto the couch. My heart felt heavy; I felt saddened by the fire chief's reaction to my confession of God sending forth His angels to spare us. I began to ponder: *Perhaps God had used me as a vessel to speak His word. Maybe the fire chief, in hearing my testimony, would begin to open his heart to the Lord so that His words would not return to Him void.*

I opened my Bible, where I immediately found solace in reading Isaiah 55:11, (NIV): "So is my word that goes out from my mouth; It will not return to me empty, but will accomplish what I desire and achieve the purpose for which I sent it."

Turning my thoughts to the angelical beings and my childish resistance to them, a barrage of shame began to overwhelm me. However, before I could indulge myself in a torrent of guilt, the Holy Spirit saturated me with a profound sense of forgiveness and understanding, to which I responded, "Hallelujah, Glory to God in the Highest, and Amen."

God Hears

Sharon Christensen

I love to read stories of answered prayer, and I've often wished God would answer a prayer of mine. Then I'd have a story to tell. But my prayers seem to be met mostly with silence.

One day I confided to a mature Christian woman and close friend of mine, "I wish I could hear God speaking to me."

She said, "If you're prompted to say a positive word or do a kindly deed, expecting nothing in return, God is speaking to you. Don't hesitate. Do it."

Encouraged by her words, my spirit lifted. Good thoughts are thoughts from God, so God does speak to me.

Months passed. As I drove to work one spring morning, my thoughts flitted like birds in the trees. *Did I remember to put rubber gloves in my bag? How busy would the market be? Would customers be attracted to still another snack line?* Then the calming, natural beauty of the country road lined with sun-dappled evergreens drew my thoughts to God.

I felt revitalized, touched by His peace. I marveled at God's amazing love and patience with me. Then a deep desire filled my soul. Thinking of the many people who would cross my path that day, I prayed aloud for only God to hear, "Please, send someone I can share your love with."

Once I arrived at the grocery store, my thoughts focused on my job. Time passed quickly while I handed out healthy snacks, answered product questions, and counted the customers who put the new snack line in their grocery carts for purchase. Looking at my watch I realized only a few minutes remained before it would be time to pack up the depleted sample supply, fold up my table, and find a dumpster for the bag of discarded plastic cups.

Shifting my weight from one foot to the other, I watched the store entry, waiting to make eye contact with another customer willing to taste samples. My eyes met the clear blue ones of a slender, attractive woman entering the super market.

Smiling, I asked, "Would you like to try a sample?"

The lady stopped in front of my table.

"These snacks are made from nuts, seeds, and a natural sweetener," I explained as I extended a tiny plastic cup containing the small snack sample.

Taking the proffered morsel, the woman surprised me by saying, "I wish I could learn more about vegetarian food and how to prepare it."

Wasting no time, for such an opportunity might be a while in coming again, I said, "I belong to a women's vegan luncheon group that meets once a month. Would you like to come?"

An eager expression lit her face, and the woman, whose name I soon learned was Ann, replied, "I'd really like that."

I explained to Ann how, each month, every member of our group cooks a favorite recipe or creates a new one and has the option of inviting a guest. As we enjoy our meal together, we have animated discussions about any number of topics—how to make a dish more simply, a connection between vegetarian food and improved health, where to find good vegetarian prepared foods and restaurants, or perhaps a personal spiritual issue.

My friend Juanita opens her home for these monthly gatherings. She's a great hostess—sets a beautiful table, makes everyone feel comfortable, and is always ready to contribute some newsy tidbit about a connection between vegetarian food and health.

A few weeks passed before the next luncheon date.

I called Ann several days in advance to tell her the time and to give her directions to Juanita's house. We chatted easily. I hung up thinking what a sweet pleasure it was to make a new friend and to introduce her to ways of preparing flavor-filled vegetarian cuisine.

Ann became a regular. As the months passed, she practiced newly acquired vegan cooking skills on us. Her self-confidence grew. She became more comfortable fixing vegetable-based dishes. She and her husband started eating plant-based soups, entrees, desserts, and whole meals. Improvement in health kept Ann asking more questions and trying more recipes.

These luncheons also give us relaxed time to visit. On one occasion, I contributed a thought from the Bible.

As we were leaving, Ann said, "I'd like to study the Bible with someone."

"Would you like to study with Juanita and me?" I asked her.

Our Bible studies soon became an important part of our lives. We meet regularly, every other week. We each bring our favorite Bible, our personal one. Indelibly imprinted in my mind are Ann's face and words the first time our Bible study group met, when she said, "I want to hear God's voice."

Tears welled in my eyes as I thought of having that same longing and of being assured by the older Christian woman that God does speak to me. I also remembered my prayer of months before: "Please, send someone for me to share Your love with."

When we meet, we bring a light lunch food to share— something we wanted to make or a vegan favorite from a local eatery. We talk about food and the health benefits of eating a vegetarian diet during lunch. Leaving dishes in the kitchen when we've finished eating, we spend the next two hours focusing on food for our souls.

At each study group, someone prays, asking the Holy Spirit for guidance, before we open God's Word. Then we read, going around the circle, stopping whenever there's a comment to make, a question, or something important to share. Often we check the margin of our Bibles and read other texts shedding light on the one being read. Many times we read two chapters, but some days only a few verses. There is no goal for the day.

Since no one has children at home, our schedules are flexible. Usually we meet at 12:30 and finish about 4:00 P.M. Bible study is an appointment that takes priority. If one of us is out of town, we wait to get together. We're spiritual sisters, and this time is sister time.

Concluding every study, we offer short prayers of commitment such as, "Lord, I want to see this challenge from your perspective."

We started by reading through the Gospel of John, one of the best-known books of the Bible. After spending almost a year studying the Book of John, we're well into the Gospel of Matthew. When we finish, we're going to read the Book of Acts to learn what God wants to teach us from the earliest Christian church.

Recently, Ann and I reflected on our meeting and our prayers: mine on the road, "Please, send someone I can share Your love with," and Ann's prayer several months previous. She told me she had stood alone on a quiet, residential street corner in town with Rex, her big German shepherd beside her, and prayed: "Dear God, please send me a new set of friends and church family; I'm far from my old ones. And teach me how to eat and live more healthfully."

Tears of joy fill Ann's eyes and mine. God hears. And He answers with heavenly timing.

A Most Important Prayer

Monica A. Andermann

"Wait a second!" my brother, Louis, called out to the hospital orderly who was wheeling him from the emergency room to the testing area. "I have to say a prayer first."

With bowed head and all due reverence, the orderly, who introduced himself as Cesar, waited as Louis said a prayer that went something like this: "Our Father who art in heaven, hallowed be Your name. Your kingdom come, now and forever. Please heal Your son, Louis. Amen."

I had gotten a phone call early that morning from the assistant manager at the community residence where Louis lives with several other special needs adults. By the urgency in his voice, I immediately knew something was wrong. In addition to having Down syndrome, Louis has also endured several surgeries to repair an improperly formed esophagus and stomach. Even the smallest gastric difficulty raises a red flag, and on this day, the assistant manager was extremely concerned with what appeared to be a severe attack of gastritis accompanied by crippling waves of abdominal pain. On the advice of his doctor, Louis had been taken by his residence aide to the hospital emergency room, and I rushed there to meet them.

As I followed the gurney, I could hear my brother continuing his soft-spoken petition. Even amidst my worry, it made me proud that Louis had the presence of mind to turn to prayer in an emergency. Our parents had always stressed to both of us that prayer is a powerful tool for healing of both mind and body. Unemployment, health issues, and relationship difficulties were regularly met with positive results through faith and prayer.

With Mom long passed and Dad too elderly to care for Louis, I had become his legal guardian—my brother's keeper. I knew that if ever there were a time to pray for him, this was it. Yet, engulfed by deep concern for him, my own prayers just wouldn't come.

As Louis was being readied in the testing suite, I sat on one of the cold metal folding chairs and closed my eyes. I hoped that, perhaps, I could at least recall one of the many Bible verses I had committed to memory through the years. But all I could see behind my darkened lids were scenes of the day replaying: Louis' face alternating between flushed and pale, his body trembling each time a new wave of pain came over him.

At the sound of footsteps approaching, I snapped open my eyes just as Cesar wheeled away the gurney on which Louis had lain only a few minutes earlier. The sight of it passing by empty made me shiver. I felt so useless; I was supposed to help and protect my brother. Now I couldn't even pray for him. Staring down at my hands, I tried in vain to keep my tears from spilling. Suddenly, I felt a touch on my shoulder.

There stood Cesar. "I liked your brother's prayer," he said. "Every morning and every night, I say a special prayer, too. Like this." He bowed his head and made the sign of the cross, "When I wake up in the morning and when I go to bed at night I say, 'Thank You, God.'"

I felt myself calm as this wise man continued, "You see, you have to remember to thank God for all the good you have now and for all the good that is to come. This is a most important prayer." With a quick nod of his head, Cesar turned and was gone.

As I continued waiting for the testing to be completed, I held on to his words like a lifeline. "Thank You, God," I repeated over and over. "Thank You for my brother.

Thank You for his health. Thank You for sending Cesar to me and giving him the right words to speak. Thank You. Thank You."

I don't know how long my brother remained in the company of scanners and X-ray machines; I was too occupied with thanking God for all His good to take notice of the time. I do know, however, that when time came for Louis to return to his bay in the emergency room, he was smiling.

As I accompanied him back to his bed, my brother reached for my hand. "I feel better," he told me and then asked if he could walk the length of the ER.

With the approval of the desk nurse, I toted his IV as he walked while his aide kept a steady hand on him. Louis returned to his bed, expelled a healthy belch, and advised us that he was feeling fine.

Within an hour, my brother was pronounced ready for discharge. The blood tests, X-rays, and scans all came back clear. Based on the evidence, there was no definitive reason why Louis should have been so ill earlier that day. The attending doctor, Louis' aide, and I all agreed that his quick recovery was nothing short of miraculous.

At his bedside, I helped my brother change from his

hospital gown into street clothes. Then together we walked out of the hospital to the curb, where the van driven by the community residence aide stood waiting for him. I helped my brother into his seat and closed the door behind him. While I watched the van grow smaller and smaller as it travelled down the long driveway, I breathed in the air of gratitude and relief. Then I, too, exhaled a most important prayer: "Thank You, God."

Mentoring Megan

Susan E. Ramsden

I have heard it said that the place where a broken bone heals ultimately becomes stronger than it was before it was injured. I believe that the same can be true for hearts.

That warm afternoon in June, as I watched Megan walk confidently across the stage at her sixth-grade graduation, I realized that although my heart wasn't exactly broken, it definitely was damaged. I wondered with a rush of both pride and pain, *Could this lovely girl, nearly a young woman now, be the same little girl who had been so timid and shy when we met so long ago?*

As her class processed down the aisle, I grinned and waved at Megan. She shot me a pained glance and hurried to join her friends at the back of the school's multipurpose room. A lump formed in my throat, and I fought back the urge to turn and leave, but I pasted a smile on my face and approached her little group.

"Congratulations, honey! I'm so proud of you," I said.

I reached out to hug her, but she stiffened and I decided against it.

Still smiling, I handed her the gifts I had carefully chosen to celebrate this milestone, and she lowered her eyes, muttering a perfunctory, "Thanks." Megan tossed the gift bag on a table, turned away, and resumed her conversation with her friends. Thus ended our six-year relationship.

I met Megan when she was a first grader at the school where I served as a reading specialist. She was a pretty little girl with large brown eyes and shiny hair that cascaded down her back in soft curls. She was always clean and appeared well cared for, but I had my concerns about her from the beginning. There was a cautious, wary quality about her that is unusual in one so young.

"What a beautiful child," I said under my breath to her teacher, Marilyn.

Marilyn frowned. "It's so sad. Megan's grandparents are raising her. Both parents are in prison. Grandma's a cold fish, and Megan's an only child. She needs more than I can give her."

My heart ached for Megan. I decided to take her under my wing that year, and she soon began to emerge from her carefully constructed cocoon. I helped her with her schoolwork, and she flourished academically. She warmed to me, began to relax, and even came to enjoy my company. We discovered a mutual love of dogs, so we often shared the antics of her beloved Chihuahua and my Bichon. She told me about her friends and school activities, but always remained guarded about her home life.

My part-time teaching position left Fridays free, so I volunteered to work with Megan on those days, as well. We looked forward to our special time together, when we shared our lives, read books about animals, wrote stories together, and worked on challenging class assignments. My daughter was away at college, and I loved having a little girl in my life again. Megan obviously enjoyed the extra attention, and her reading and writing scores increased under my tutelage. Megan's artistic ability became evident, too, so I began to haunt art and craft stores in search of sales on paints, art paper, clay, and craft kits.

Our workspace, a tiny teachers' workroom nestled between two bustling classrooms, wasn't ideal. A window in the door afforded curious little passersby a chance to peek in at our activities, which seemed to annoy and perhaps even embarrass Megan at times. We were happy, though, to have a quiet place to work and enjoy each other's company.

I'll never forget the day I pulled out an acrylic paint set from my bag. Megan's big eyes grew even bigger. "Wow! What's that?"

"Watch," I said and squeezed a dot of burnt umber onto the plastic palette, swirling it into a dot of titanium white.

"Cool! Let me try!" she giggled, taking the plastic mixing knife from me.

I slid a canvas board across to her. "Now, sweetie, you can paint like Monet!"

Megan touched my hand in an uncharacteristic show of affection, and she set to work daubing and mixing a kaleidoscope of colors onto her palette. Her quizzical smile spread into a full-fledged grin as she swiped her brush across the canvas. It's the happiest I ever saw her, and I felt my eyes well with gratitude.

Over the next few years, it was a delight to watch Megan become a more confident and outgoing girl who had a sparkle in her eyes and a spring in her step. At first, I thought of my work with Megan as a ministry, but before long I began to think of her more as a second daughter.

Even after I retired, I continued to mentor Megan. I had been offered the opportunity to substitute and tutor children for pay, but that would have meant having to renege on my commitment to Megan. I decided that this child was more important than supplementing the family income.

Despite my efforts to stay connected, though, by the end of her fifth grade year, I noticed that Megan had begun to distance herself from me. By the sixth grade, it was obvious she had lost interest in her schoolwork, artwork, and in spending time with me. Megan smiled less, and her shiny-eyed enthusiasm had faded. I was saddened when I realized that she had begun to skip school.

Many Fridays when I arrived at Megan's classroom, I was greeted with, "She's absent again." Eventually, I realized that Megan must be playing hooky to avoid our time together. When I tried to discuss the problem with her teacher, she shrugged in discouragement and resignation.

"Grandma won't return my calls," she said. "Megan's grades are plummeting. She's going to slip through the cracks. Soon she'll be just another statistic."

There was little I could do, other than pray and continue to support her when she was with me. Her sullen expression and monotone greeting made me wonder if I was wasting my time on this moody preteen who now shunned all attempts at help and friendship. The temptation was to turn and walk away, but knowing that she had recently lost her grandfather, I realized this child needed me more than ever. I asked God to give me the grace to stay the course.

I will never know what caused Megan to wall off her heart from me. Perhaps our friendship became an embarrassment to her as she got older. Her friends may have teased her about being taken out of the classroom. There may have been things going on at home that were too difficult to talk about, which may have colored her attitude toward life.

One dreary, overcast morning, I drove along the coast to my favorite spot at the beach to seek the Lord. On a cliff high above the crashing surf, while rays of sunlight attempted to pierce the gloom, I prayed for comfort and guidance to deal with my feelings about this child, whom I had come to love. I couldn't help but think how much our relationship had become like our Heavenly Father's relationship with each of us. From the beginning of human history, He has longed to interact with His children in deep and meaningful ways . . . to care for us . . . to guide us . . . to share His bounty with us . . . to redeem us and draw us to Him . . . and to love and be loved in return. From the beginning, many have resisted His attempts at reconciliation. Many have chosen instead to run from His outstretched arms, preferring independence over His perfect parenting, searching for love and meaning everywhere but in Him. I realized then that the Lord knew exactly what I was going through and was with me in the struggle.

Sometimes I think God tests our mettle by calling us to love the resistant or unlovable ones. I believe that He asks us to learn to love unconditionally, to give without expecting anything in return. I realized this was my time to rise above my own self-interests and injured feelings. I persevered with Megan throughout her elementary school career, and I'm glad that I did, even though it ended poorly. I hope that, ultimately, I made some kind of a positive impact on this young girl who had experienced so much loss. Perhaps through the telescope of time she has been able to discover my love for her and to realize that I had her best interests at heart.

Megan is grown now, and our paths have never again crossed. The day of her sixth-grade graduation was the last time I saw her. One of my gifts to her that day was a journal in which I wrote of my appreciation for her many fine qualities and my gratitude for the privilege of befriending her. I still think of Megan and hope that she is happy and fulfilled. My fervent prayer for her is that she will come to know our matchless Mentor, the Lord Jesus Christ, who will befriend her, protect her, guide her, and love her in the unquenchable, unfathomable ways that I and her family could not.

I know that I grew and matured from having this little girl in my life. Through mentoring Megan, the Lord taught me that love and kindness are never wasted. They bless the one who receives as well as the one who gives. I believe that I am a little stronger and my heart is a little bigger for having loved someone who didn't, in the end, return my love.

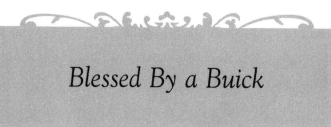

Blessed By a Buick

Anne Magee Dichele

A few years back, I was hit by a car . . . while jogging, on vacation. A friend and I were about three miles into an early morning run, enjoying the serene beauty of Nantucket Island. Nantucket is twenty miles off the coast of Massachusetts, an island which in off-season (it was April) is as pristinely quiet as it is beautiful. We were jogging along Bartlett Farm Road, a long, flat stretch of asphalt, cushioned on either side by rows and rows of lettuce, zinnias, and strawberries in summer. But in April, the earthy richness of freshly tilled soil is so strong you can taste it. It is a beautifully barren area, cool and damp with dense fog and sea-salt winds; the farm ripe with endless acres of soon-to-flourish vegetation; utterly quiet; wonderfully desolate.

I have been a runner for years, and most of my running occurs in cities—Boston, where I grew up; New Haven, where I live currently. I dodge cars, trucks, and buses without incident. But put me on a desolate farm road on an island far from civilization—and *whack*!

I now know what people mean when they say, "It happened so fast, I didn't know what hit me," because for a split second, I truly had no idea why one moment I was jogging along talking with my friend and the next moment I was thrown skyward, my legs clipped sharply from behind, both right and left calf muscles crying out together, exploding in pain.

As quickly as I was thrown upward, I came down to earth—hard. I landed flat on my behind but leaning fully forward, as if I were attempting to stretch out and touch my toes. I tried to sit up and only then realized that the front end of a rather imposing Buick LeSabre, circa 1976, was now parked over my back.

I turned my neck slowly to the left. Staring back at me, mirrored in the shiny grill of the massive front-end, were about twelve reflections of my face, each grimacing in the lines of chrome, like those silly funhouse mirrors that distort your image and make your head look like a cucumber and your body a pumpkin.

Adrenaline is a great drug. Get hit by a car, and momentarily you feel giddy with fear and relief. Here I was, practically kissing my own knees, lying beneath a Buick, and I felt fine. Really. My jogging partner, meanwhile, was about to have a stroke, having watched the entire incident from less than a foot away. She immediately began to freak out, screaming at the driver, screaming at me. I tried to reassure her while attempting to extricate myself from under the front end of the car, grateful that I was able to bend far enough forward that I avoided being crushed. I shimmied out, held on to the front fender, and stood up, still giggling slightly from embarrassment and relief.

Wobbly, but in one piece, I placed my hands on the hood of the car to make sure my legs worked before giving them my full weight. Only then did I notice the Buick had a driver, frozen behind the wheel. The driver was old. She had one of those tiny, shrunken faces, and her forehead wasn't even level with the top of the massive steering wheel. No wonder she'd slammed into me; she couldn't possibly see anything through the windshield. She appeared to be ashen with disbelief, grasping onto the steering wheel with, I kid you not, white-gloved hands.

For a brief second I thought, *Perhaps I'm in some kind of weird dream. Who gets hit by a car in Nantucket? And who wears white driving gloves? Actually, who wears white gloves at all anymore?*

My friend, now entirely frantic, tried to pierce through my dazed and what must have appeared extremely bizarre giggling by screaming at me: "Annie! Are you alright? Annie! Annie!"

"I'm okay. But the old lady behind the wheel looks like she may have had a heart attack." I smiled, a weak attempt to lighten up the moment.

Suddenly, a man pedaled up to us on a bicycle—a tall, thin, muscular, Lance Armstrong–type of character, helmet strapped tightly under his chin, calf muscles bulging from below his Lycra bike shorts. *Nice legs*, I thought, still dazed. Meanwhile, my own legs felt like they had been hollowed out and filled with quick-dry cement.

The bicyclist was hyperventilating with disbelief. "I saw everything! She ran right off the road and into you! Veered right off and hit you! I saw her do it!"

As the Lance Armstrong guy stood astride his bicycle, arms flailing for emphasis, I grinned at him stupidly, still steadying myself, palms flat on the hood of the Buick.

The driver, from what I could see of her, was still frozen to the wheel. For a brief moment, I remember fearing she may have died there, grasping the steering wheel. When

I looked again, past my friend and the biker man, I saw she was still clutching the wheel with her white gloves, unmoved but blinking occasionally, clearly still alive.

"Go see if she's okay, will you?" I asked my friend. "I'm fine. Really."

For the record, I always say "I'm fine," especially when I am really not fine. I am unsure why I do this, but it must be some genetic form of stoicism, because my older sister and my younger brother both do the same thing. A response of "I'm fine" in my family translates into, "You know that I am really not fine at all, but I am too embarrassed or ashamed or emotionally repressed about this to talk about it."

Anyhow, my running partner, who also understands the "I'm fine" thing, went to help the driver, knowing full well that I might collapse at any minute but also knowing it was useless to try and help me once the "I'm fine" had been uttered. So she went to the driver's side door and opened it. The biker man continued to gesture his disbelief at the situation.

With my friend's assistance, the diminutive driver finally emerged from behind the wheel. She was indeed tiny, perhaps five feet, maybe less. But she was wonderfully dignified for what was clearly an undignified moment. She stood beside the car, shaken but elegant in her ironed and neatly creased khaki pants and a starched white-collared shirt open at the neckline, revealing mottled skin that had been browned and weathered from, I presumed, many years of Nantucket's offshore winds. She was a miniature Katherine Hepburn, craggy with age and yet holding herself as tall as she could, chin up, with style. I liked her right away.

The gloves, on closer inspection, appeared to be more garden gloves than formal gloves, more beige canvas than white cotton. She must have been gardening earlier, before this fateful drive to Bartlett's Farm.

By now, I was feeling a little nauseous. I also started to worry about Ms. Hepburn, who began to tremble uncontrollably, her moment of distinguished elegance disintegrating as she drew nearer. She looked at me helplessly as the biker man admonished her.

"What were you thinking?" he railed. "You just drove right into her! What were you thinking?"

I was beginning to really dislike Lance Armstrong, nice legs or no.

"Look, I am fine. Everything is fine," I said, hoping Lance would get the hint that I wanted him and his bicycle to move along. I smiled weakly at Ms. Hepburn.

The biker man shoved a ragged piece of paper at me. "Here's my name and number if you need a witness. Call me any time."

I limply took the paper, grateful to watch the thin racing wheels of his bike spinning away down the desolate road.

"Should we call the police?" Ms. Hepburn said in a small voice.

I didn't have a cell phone, and neither did my friend. I figured that Ms. Hepburn probably didn't either, given the vintage of her Buick.

"No. Let's exchange information, just in case," I said, without wanting to think what that might be. But, of course, I had nothing to write with or on—after all, we'd been running.

"Do you have a pen or anything?"

Ms. Hepburn opened the glove compartment of her car, reached in and presented me with a small, white business card. It was embossed simply with the name "Mrs. Norton A. Smith." That's it. No phone, no email address, just a name. I looked at it.

"It's my calling card," she explained, as if everyone had one nowadays. "We're in the Nantucket phone book. I live on Milk Street, in town."

After a few more assurances that everyone was fine, Mrs. Norton A. Smith drove away, very slowly. Perhaps she was expecting her car to veer directly into another jogging duo; perhaps she was simply scared to death at the thought of what could have happened. I know I was.

I limped home. It took until sunset for the blue and purple bruises that covered both my calves to really blossom into deep eggplant-black reminders of my morning encounter with a Buick. But the real pain started about two days later, every time I sat for more than ten minutes. A dull ache at the very base of my spine wouldn't go away, and for a week or two I thought it was just residual soreness. After finally seeing a doctor (which all my friends rightly admonished me for not doing sooner), I learned I had a hairline fracture of my tailbone. Nothing really of concern, the doctor assured me, except that it would be nearly six months before I could sit for more than ten minutes without feeling the dull ache return.

I don't know what ever happened to Mrs. Norton A. Smith. I never saw her, never spoke to her again. In retrospect, I know I should have done something: contacted the authorities; put people on notice that Mrs. Norton A. Smith was a potential danger to others. But I didn't.

After safely making our way back to the cottage that fateful morning, I sent everyone into town, feigning the need for quiet and rest. Then I crept out onto the back deck, wrapped my calves in bags of ice, and cried . . . and cried . . . and cried. I sat weeping for the entire afternoon, alone, dripping in ice packs, and soaking my sweatshirt with tears I had swallowed for years.

Sitting on that back deck, I admitted to myself for the first time in twenty years that my marriage, my life, my family were in shambles. I was deeply unhappy. I had begun to hate the person I had become. My husband was an addict and seriously unstable, and I had spent the last ten years of my life pretending not to notice. My children were anxious and afraid most of the time, and I was exhausted.

For months after the incident, my friends and family wanted me to file a lawsuit against Mrs. Norton A. Smith. I never did. I told those who chided me most that I didn't believe in promoting a more litigious society, or that I wasn't seriously hurt, or that my compassion would be rewarded by others' compassion toward me in the future. But in truth, the main reason I didn't pursue a lawsuit was because I could barely get up in the morning in the months following getting hit. The floodlight of scrutiny this accident had shed on my marriage and my life was nearly unbearable.

What I know now that I did not realize then is that sometimes God literally has to catapult us into the truth. I laugh now, when I think about God looking down from heaven, shaking his head, and saying to Himself, "I'm actually going to have to hit her with a Buick to get her to think straight!"

Thank you, Lord. And thank you, Mrs. Norton A. Smith, if you are reading this. I don't know how long it would have taken me to see the truth of my life without you slamming into me with your car, but I am glad you did. My life, unlike my injuries, began to heal that day. The pain continues sometimes; damp days can still make my backside ache. But most days when people ask, "How are you?" I can honestly say, "I'm fine."

Milk for Babies and a Golden Calf

Tami Absi

The scent of lilac shampoo filled the living room as Mother went to fetch the big-toothed, blue comb Dad won at last year's fair. Grandma's skirt huffed at the hem when she plopped in the kitchen chair in front of the walnut-framed, four-panel picture window. Her legs were too short for her to sit gracefully; from my seat on the floor, I could see her flesh-colored garters pretending to hide under her rolled up hose-tops just above her knees. I smoothed my dress over my bent knees. It wasn't right to sit "Injun style" in front of Grandma. She'd told me more than once that she didn't want to see my panties until jammie time.

"Grandma," I asked, "why don't you cut your hair? Bangs keep the hair outta my eyes."

Grandma answered with a tone as sweet as the peppermint candy in her mouth. "It's in the King James. A woman's hair is her glory. It's written down. God expects us to use our hair as a covering. No woman at my church needs to wear a hankie on her head."

Mother smiled the smile grownups often wore behind Grandma's back. It should have been named the "Grandma Opinion Smirk." Sometimes the smile came with a wink or a nod, and when they forgot themselves, they bold-faced smiled like that right in front of her. When my parents, uncles, and aunts talked behind Grandma's back, they said she knew her Bible but she didn't understand that times change.

Mother separated Grandma's silver hair into sections, and she began to comb each section way down—past the last scroll-cut on the leg of the kitchen chair.

Smoothing the first section, Mother said, "The Bible also says God numbers the hair on our heads. Looks like you might be making God's job more difficult."

My family took the Bible seriously, but they also played with it. They threw verses around the room like darts . . . while I searched for the target. I wondered if God winked behind their backs.

The sun's westerly pink rays blushed in Grandma's silvery strands, sparkling brighter and dancing faster as the warm energy dried her hair. After Mother smoothed Grandma's hair into a twisted luminous bun, the kitchen chair was returned and the table was set for four. Dad joined us for dinner, a meat-and-potatoes meal the way Grandma liked it, and I anticipated a night alone with Grandma. I wanted to ask her something about meat and potatoes.

Finally, my parents dressed and left for the evening. Grandma played her autoharp, and I knew the words because Dad sang them in the church choir:

My heart can sing
As I pause to remember
A heartache here is but a stepping stone
A long life's trail that's always winding upward,
For this old world is not my final home. . . .

The heartache part of the song caused me to consider my meat-and-potatoes question. During jammie time, I asked, "Grandma, Mother said that during the Great Depression you only had raw potatoes to eat most nights."

She spun me around so she could unbutton my dress. "It was our time of wandering through the wilderness."

I pulled up my pajama pants. "Why did you eat them raw?"

Her lips broadened into a squinting smile, and her eyes did the same. She rooted for another peppermint from her pocket. "People didn't have things. Sometimes we didn't have the wood for the stove. We couldn't cook the potatoes without wood. In the summer, cooking them made the house hot. The potatoes were like manna. Manna isn't supposed to taste good; it's supposed to sustain a body. Just sustain."

"Mother said other people in the neighborhood had more 'cause they took welfare."

Grandma slipped the pajama top over hands I held high like the people in church sometimes did, but they weren't getting dressed. "Yep. Your Uncle Wilbur, my oldest monkey, worked at the shop making wood tool boxes, so on Friday, we had meat. I didn't take handouts, even though I had one little, one middle-sized, and one grown monkey to feed. I was raising them alone, because your grandfather died before the Depression. I babysat for the women who worked in the factory. They wanted younger women in the factory."

"But why didn't you take the welfare, at least take the food?"

Grandma pulled back my covers and followed me into

bed. "I'll rest with you until you fall asleep," she said. "In the wilderness, you aren't supposed to have a fatted calf. Why do you think God got so mad at the Israelites in the wilderness when they made the golden calf?" Grandma allowed her head to sink into the pillow. "Enough talking. Time for sleep."

As I nestled my head in the pillow, I realized I was now wearing the Grandma Opinion Smirk on my face. "But my Sunday school teacher said the golden calf had something to do with worshipping other gods."

"The only real help you'll find in this world comes from above. In some situations, you could argue it's right to take what you can find where you can find it," Grandma said soothingly. "After your mother married, everyone used rationing stamps for milk and such, but your mother gave the milk stamps to the neighbors with babies. Your mother was kind to the neighbors, a good witness. Maybe what God wanted in your mother's neighborhood wasn't what he needed in mine. I sought after righteousness in my time."

Then she turned her head and closed her eyes like she did when she sang hymns. "You need to go to sleep," she murmured.

I closed my eyes, but one question seemed to unravel

another. I knew Grandma never got mad. Not at me. Never at anyone. So, pretending to yawn, I asked, "What's the difference between right and righteous?"

"A person can argue they're right. They can prove it in a court of law. Only God can decide what's righteous, and sometimes He whispers words right into your heart if you're listening. Those words are just between the two of you. Go to sleep," she said with a real yawn.

"But how do I know it isn't the devil talkin'?"

"You know the answer. If it breaks the Ten Commandments, it isn't God. And I said God whispers in your heart. If you ever start hearing voices in your head, you need to tell somebody," she said with a chuckle. "Sleep, now, grandmonkey."

I closed my eyes, and images of milk for babies, manna, meat, potatoes, fatted calves, and a golden one danced across my mind. I fell asleep trying to decide which ones were wrong, which ones were right, and which ones were righteous in my neighborhood.

When I married, my husband and I rented a house, and the previous renters left behind a large, burgeoning garden. Before unpacking all the boxes, I knocked on the neighbors' doors and invited them to come pick whatever they wanted.

I wasn't without, I wasn't rationed, and I knew what God wanted in my neighborhood. He didn't even have to whisper it in my heart. Grandma's lesson had suffused my soul.

A Time to Dance

Teresa Brady

This past summer my four-year-old grandson, Dallas, vacationed with my husband and me for nearly five weeks. How quickly I had forgotten the time it takes to get a preschooler out the door each day, especially on Sunday mornings. I knew that Sunday mornings were going to be particularly difficult, because my husband was a minister, and I would have the task of bringing my grandson, along with all his belongings, to church by myself. It would be a one-woman show, and I had not played this role in a very long time. Surely, though, after raising his mother and her sister, one little boy wouldn't be too difficult to manage? (Yes, the memory is one of the first things to go!)

Our first Sunday morning arrived, and I found myself running around frantically trying to get everything packed and organized for a preschooler in tow. How quickly I'd forgotten all the things needed, such as clothing changes, snacks, and favorite toys. The list seemed to go on and on. I was so preoccupied with my list that, I have to admit,

I barely noticed my grandson scampering near my feet as I passed him in the hallway near my bedroom.

Suddenly, there he was, directly below me in the doorway. At first, I nearly brushed right past him, but as I looked toward him, his actions brought me to a dead stop. Dallas was looking up at me with those astonishingly blue eyes and his arms reaching straight upward.

"Grandma, let's dance," he said. I must say it caught me off-guard for a second when he went on to say, "Grandma, you look beautiful in that dancing dress."

My heart melted. I hadn't thought about what I looked like or even what I had put on that day. If truth be told, I wasn't into the moment, just into the task ahead.

Then and there, I made a decision that affected the rest of my day and, I imagine, the rest of my life: take the time to dance. Putting aside the many things on my list, I stopped and danced in the doorway with my four-year-old grandson as if I didn't have anything more urgent to do. And honestly, I *didn't* have anything more important to do. Yes, I felt beautiful, too!

The sweetness of the moment took my breath away. But what Dallas said next utterly blew me away.

"Grandma, after we get to church, you need to tell Pa

that he needs to stop working or whatever he is doing and just dance with you."

"Why?" I asked.

Dallas looked up at me again and, smiling from ear to ear, said, "Because, Grandma, you are just beautiful in that dancing dress."

This is unbelievable, I thought to myself. *He gets it. My four-year-old grandson understands what is most essential.*

Work will always be present. Lists will continue to reproduce themselves. Projects will never end. But moments will not last. People will not always remain. And dances are to be danced!

On that Sunday morning when I was rushing around and worrying about being on time, oblivious to a beautiful moment standing right in front of me, Dallas reminded me of one of our Lord's greatest lessons on living, as stated in Ecclesiastes 3:1–4 (NIV):

1   There is a time for everything,
    and a season for every activity under heaven:
2   a time to be born and a time to die,
    a time to plant and a time to uproot,

3 a time to kill and a time to heal,
    a time to tear down and a time to build,
4 a time to weep and a time to laugh,
    a time to mourn and a time to dance,

I pray that my grandson, Dallas, will always enjoy the dance of life. That he will always take the time to stop and enjoy the beautiful moments with which God graces each and every day. And that I will get to see him raise his outstretched arms to his new bride, look into her eyes with those astonishing blue eyes of his, and say, "You look beautiful today. Let's dance."

A version of this story was first published in *Mature Living*, August 2009.

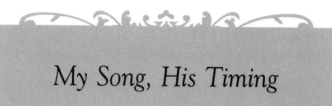

My Song, His Timing

Mary C. M. Phillips

"What do you want me to do?" I asked.

Then louder, with some frustration: "*What do you want me to do?!*"

I was talking to God. In prayer. My kind of prayer. See, my prayers are audible, as if I'm talking to someone in the room. Someone who is actually listening to my venting. (I promise you, I only do this when I'm alone.)

I had not felt the presence of peace in several months. Nothing out of the ordinary had been going on in my life, though. Nothing had changed. That was the weird thing. I just had the sense that I should be doing something— what, I didn't know. The feeling had been particularly strong the day before at work. As I sat at my desk, I was overcome with the feeling that I should be doing something else. Something other than entering contacts into Microsoft Outlook for my boss. Something purposeful. Something good.

For a while, I also had felt a pressure in my chest that

I can only explain as a weight on my heart. A spiritual hunger. Although it was not physical, it was very real.

I prayed long and hard to hear His voice. I sought advice from friends, who would say, "Be patient and wait upon The Lord." I know that patience is a virtue, one I didn't have. But I trusted in those words, as painful and draining as that sometimes was.

Eventually, my spirit seemed to say, "Enough already, Mary!" and I made a move. Not a conscious move, but a move all the same. While I was at work one day entering some random name into my boss's contacts, he sharply corrected my entry, and I just looked up and said, "I quit."

Did I feel a sense of relief when I walked out of the office? No! Not in the least. It was more like sheer panic. What did I just do? I needed to make money and pay my bills! Was the pressure in my heart gone? Well, maybe a bit. But, really, what was I accomplishing?

The next morning I woke up still feeling slightly confused. Before leaving for work, my husband kissed me goodbye and assured me that we'd be fine; we'd figure something out. As I sipped my coffee, feeling thankful for my husband's reaction, I noticed that the same pressure I had been trying to shake was still with me.

That's when I asked God, "What do you want from me?" That's when I prayed out loud, "What do you want me to do?"

For some reason, my attention was drawn to my piano. I had spent a number of years as a musician but hadn't played in a long time. Desperate to understand and to feel at peace again, I figured anything was worth a try. So I asked (again, out loud, 'cause that's just how I pray), "Do you want me to play music? Do you want me to write a song?"

I got off my butt. (This is a very important step in changing one's life, by the way.) I got off my butt and walked over to the piano. I sat down on the piano bench, and I said out loud and in a very matter-of-fact tone, "Okay. If you want me to write a song, put it in my fingers."

Then I just started playing and singing, "I've got Jesus in my heart showing me the way. . . ."

It was good. The entire song was good. I played it again just to make sure.

I called my husband and played it for him over the phone. He liked it.

Still not quite trusting, I asked my husband if he'd ever heard the song before. I worried whether I had unintentionally ripped it off. He assured me he'd never heard it before. "It's good," he said.

After we hung up, I played the song again and suddenly noticed that the weight in my heart had been lifted. The hunger in my spirit was gone. It was weird and wonderful at the same time.

To make a long story short, I recorded the song, "Jesus in My Heart," with my husband (also a musician) and some other musician friends. I printed up CDs and put it on iTunes, like most musicians do today. Then I just left it alone.

I went back to work one day a week (with the same boss, now apologetic) and began my life of writing. Today, I write songs, short stories, and poems. I now have a purpose, and I am acutely aware of walking in His will. My spirit is no longer hungry. It's been quenched, and I am thankful that the Holy Spirit guides us all in mysterious ways and in His own timing.

Recently, I watched a video on YouTube. It is a clip of about 100 orphan children in Swaziland, Africa. They stand in a circle, barefoot in the dirt. This is their church. The worship leader, Laura Hawthorne, is leading the children in a song. She smiles at the camera as the music starts.

Then, joyfully and beautifully, the children begin singing: "I've got Jesus in my heart showing me the way. . . ."

They are singing my song. His song. And all in His perfect timing.

My Cross, His Cross

Helena Solano

It is Holy Thursday, and I don't know why, but I'm drawn to this small Catholic church tucked away on the edge of campus. It's evening, the sun is setting, and I see lights glowing softly through the stained glass. I've walked by this small chapel quite a few times as a student on campus, but for the first time, I go in. I sit in the back, the far back, where it's dark and I'm hoping no one will talk to me or, for that matter, even notice that I'm here or alive.

I am not a churchgoer. In fact, what I really am is angry at God. I'm angry over all the hard stuff that has happened in my life—my father's alcoholism, the constant verbal and physical abuse, the estrangement from my siblings, my mother's cancer, and a loneliness so deep I think it's going to kill me. I have so much I am angry over.

Going in and sitting down, I wonder if there really is a God who cares about me or knows everything about me. I wonder how there could be a God who is concerned about me or knows about me after all I've seen and been through.

But for some reason I am drawn here this Thursday, the holiest Thursday of the year for Christians across the globe. As I walk in, others are walking in as well. I see a table set up in the front of the church; it is long, covered in a smooth white cloth, and set for twelve people. The twelve people sitting at the table include men and women, young and old, black and white. And the priest, Father Tom.

I hear the voice of the man sitting at the head of the table saying, "Come in. Welcome! Come on in. There's room for you at this table. Come to the feast of the Lord, where all are welcome."

For some reason, sitting in the back, hiding in the shadows, I feel the honesty and the sincerity of Father Tom's words, and I feel welcomed.

I decide to go back the next day, Good Friday, and even then, I don't think there is anything this priest can say that will undo the pain and hurt I feel. My heart feels crusted over, like a wound that has never been properly treated or cared for.

When I arrive for the evening service on that Good Friday, I notice a wooden cross in the front. It is large, dark brown, rough, and empty. Father Tom is in the front, and this time I listen. He is talking about crosses, and I have never heard anyone talk about crosses this way. He says that we all have crosses in our lives, and he talks about Jesus' death on the cross, of his pain. But I'm so stuck in my own pain that Jesus' suffering really isn't meaning much to me in that moment because all I can feel is my suffering.

Suddenly and quietly, Father Tom reaches into his cassock and pulls out a small wooden cross. The dark brown color of the cross against his white cassock strikes me, and I am keenly aware of Father Tom's words. As he holds that small, wooden cross in front of his chest, he says, "This is my cross. What's yours?"

His words cut me, and my crusted, angry, hard heart breaks wide open in that dark student chapel, and I begin to weep.

Father Tom goes on, talking about God's pain and our pain. That they are the same pain, and Jesus carried our pain on his cross. That what Jesus really wanted was to carry our pain for us and with us. And that, come what may, we are never alone.

Just as suddenly and quietly as Father Tom pulled the cross from his cassock, my pain—which is everything and nothing, which has broken and crusted and angered and hardened my heart—comes into view. I feel those words deep within where I thought nothing could ever go again, and I know my life will never be the same after this night.

As I weep, those words, "This is my cross. What's your cross?" echo through my soul over and over again. Father Tom stands there holding that cross in front of him for a while, and all the pain I've been feeling for years comes together in that moment. A culmination of all the wounds, and fears, and hurts, and deep loneliness come together, and I know for the first time in a very long time that I am loved and not alone in my pain. I know that God is really not bothered or put off by my anger.

For years I had wanted to die, and I contemplated suicide many times, but weeping on my knees in that dark chapel, I knew with every cell in my body that God was with me and that the Jesus who hung on the cross did so to join me in my suffering. I felt wrapped in the arms of Jesus and knew His cross was now a part of my cross. I didn't know how, but I knew I could go on with my life now. At that moment, I knew God *got* it—my pain, my loneliness, my sorrow, my suffering, even my anger were not unfamiliar to Him. Somehow, I knew there was more to my life than the sad story it had been until then. I didn't know what that other story was, but I knew God had more for my life then the path behind me. I knew I was meant to live.

More than two decades, three degrees, a husband of twenty years, and two wonderful children later, I remember that night clearly—when my cross became one with His cross.

Step by slow step, my life did change. It took years of work to overcome the pain and loneliness I'd felt all those dark years. It took years to undo the cruelty of my childhood, the fear of my teenage years, and the loneliness of my early adulthood. I often wondered if the sun would ever shine in my soul and if I would ever be whole. But that day did come—carried on the promise I heard on that Good Friday in that small chapel on that night of nights. That my cross is His cross. That I am never alone. That He is always here with me. That His love and his compassion are everlasting.

Contributors

Tami Absi ("Milk for Babies and a Golden Calf") lives in Dayton, Ohio, and teaches English to eleventh and twelfth graders. Her writing has been published in *Mock Turtle Zine*, *A Cup of Comfort® for Couples*, and online news venues. She is happily married with two lovely children, Josh and Jackie.

Sandy Adams ("The Life That Almost Wasn't") has been writing, speaking to women's groups, and teaching marriage seminars for over twenty years. She and her husband of thirty-nine years reside in Georgetown, Texas. She has one son and four grandchildren. Sandy's passion is finding and sharing the beauty and joy of each new day.

Monica A. Andermann ("A Living Lesson" and "A Most Important Prayer") is a freelance writer who lives on Long Island with her husband, Bill, and their cat, Charley. When she is not writing, she most enjoys reading or spending time with family and friends. Her work has been widely published both online and in a variety of print media, including several credits in the *Cup of Comfort®* book series and other anthologies.

Nancy Antonietti ("Blessed Mothers") is a retired engineer who has given up design of experiments in favor of crafting dialogue and spinning narrative. She lives in New Hampshire but dreams of moving to Sicily. While caring for her family and learning to quilt, she is currently working on a novel. Her writing has been honored by PEN Nob Hill and Seacoast Writers and published in various magazines as well as in *A Cup of Comfort® for the Grieving Heart*.

Teresa Brady ("A Time to Dance") is passionate about spending time with her grandson, writing, working in women's ministry, and working alongside her husband in ministry for over thirty years.

Nancy Brewka-Clark ("The Other Cheek") lives with her husband, Tom, in Beverly, Massachusetts. Themes of hope and redemption have inspired many of her more than five-hundred published nonfiction articles, short stories, poems, and plays.

AnneRené Capp ("Did You Say Angels?") is the pen name of an impassioned freelance writer and poet who feels motivated to uplift the hearts of her readers and considers the Bible to be her tool of precision. A lifelong resident of Northern California, she enjoys all genres of writing but is especially fond of humor—per Proverbs 22:17: "A merry heart doeth good like a medicine: but a broken spirit drieth the bones."

Priscilla Carr ("Love Is a Christian Verb"), memoirist and poet, is founder of The Poet's Studio of New Hampshire. Her prose appears in Adams Media's *Cup of Comfort*® and *Hero*® book series, and her poetry in *It Has Come to This: Poets of the Great Mother Conference* and *Grandmother's Necklace*. She is a mentoree of Robert Bly and Donald Hall.

Sharon Christensen ("God Hears"), a professional food writer, ACF-certified executive chef, and vegan, delights in experimenting with food, creating recipes, and sharing plant-based dishes with her family and friends. She and her husband, Don, own a health food store, Nature's Food Center, and a vegan restaurant, Nature's Bounty, in Lakeport, California.

Sally Clark ("Roller Coaster of Faith) and her husband live in Fredericksburg, Texas, with their two grown children and five grandchildren all living nearby. Sally began writing when they retired from their restaurant in 2001. Her award-winning stories and poems for adults and children have been widely published. She also writes greeting cards, devotionals, nonfiction, and humor.

Anne Magee Dichele ("Blessed By a Buick") is a professor at Quinnipiac University in Connecticut, a published poet, and a writer of stories for adults and children. She lives in New Haven and is blessed with two wonderful sons, a loving family, amazing friends, and most important, a deep faith in God's unending care for each of us.

Debora Dyess ("The Hobbyhorse Miracle") still attends Southside Baptist church, where she is a member of the children's ministry team. Now a grandmother and full-time writer, Debora is published in several anthologies and is editor for bellaonline's News for Kids site. She still plans things out for God and is constantly amazed at His better plan.

Shawnelle Eliasen ("Personal Hannah") and her husband, Lonny, live in Illinois. They have five sons, and Shawnelle home teaches the three youngest. She began writing two years ago and has been published in *Guideposts*, *Mom Sense*, *Marriage Partnership*, and anthologies such as *A Cup of Comfort® for Couples*, *Christmas Spirit*, *Praying from the Heart*, and others.

Patricia Fish ("The Only Thing That Matters"), of Georgetown, Delaware, is retired and busy in her church. She also enjoys blogging, gardening, painting, and being a grandmother.

Judy Gerlach ("Shirley, Goodness, and Mercy") works for her husband, Greg's, video-production company in Lexington, Kentucky. A published author of church drama, she began her writing career writing plays and sketches for her church. Judy's nonfiction work has been published in two of Adams Media's *Hero®* series anthologies as well as in *A Cup of Comfort® for Fathers*.

Leann Guzman ("This Broken Vessel") is an attorney who lives near Fort Worth, Texas. She is a happy wife and frugal mom of three as well as an avid reader, aspiring gardener, occasional writer, frequent cook, and blessed child of God.

Taryn R. Hutchison ("Worth the Wait") is the author of *We Wait You: Waiting on God in Eastern Europe* and has published stories in two other anthologies. Taryn served on staff with Campus Crusade for Christ for many years, later working at Golden Gate Seminary. She and her husband recently relocated to western North Carolina.

Jennie Ivey ("Bless These Reckless Drivers") lives in Cookeville, Tennessee. She is a newspaper columnist and the author of three books—*Tennessee Tales the Textbooks Don't Tell, E Is for Elvis,* and *Soldiers, Spies, and Spartans*—and various other fiction and nonfiction works. She and her husband, George, are the parents of three grown children.

Marsha Mott Jordan ("His Night Watch Care") is a humor and inspirational writer and speaker, the mother of a grown son, and the grandmother of a little boy who is the joy of her life. She lives with lupus, her rocket-scientist husband of nearly three decades, and a toy poodle named King Louie in the north woods of Wisconsin. After her grandson was badly burned, she founded Hugs and Hope, a nonprofit organization dedicated to cheering critically ill and injured children. She is the author of the essay collection *Hugs, Hope, and Peanut Butter*, which is illustrated by children battling for life.

Kathryn Lay ("A Walking Testimony" and "Twice Blessed") lives in Texas with her husband, daughter, and two dogs. She and her husband help lead a training school for young future missionaries. She is a full-time writer, author, and speaker for children and adults.

Mitsie McKellick ("God and the Radio") lives in Mechanic Falls, Maine. She and her husband, Tim, recently began pastoring a Vineyard Church in nearby Naples, Maine. They have five children and one grandchild. Mitsie enjoys gardening, arts and crafts, writing for a local newspaper, and telling stories.

Jennifer Mersberger ("A Perfect Fit") is the founder of Lamplight Ministry. As a public speaker and author, Jennifer encourages the hearts of women. Her Bible study, *Parables of the Master Storyteller*, equips readers with God's Word in their daily lives. She and her family live in Newark, Texas, where she is an avid scrapbooker.

Katrina Norfleet ("Released") is a mother, author, and Life Purpose Coach® who makes her living as a marketing communications writer but feeds her soul writing fiction and creative nonfiction from her home in Maryland. Her work appears in the *Victorious Living for Women* anthology, *Our Voices* at *www.BoomerWomenSpeak*, various magazines, and her blog, Joy-Filled Life.

Galen Pearl ("A Mustard Seed of Faith") is the pen name of a Southern girl transplanted to the Pacific Northwest, where she is a full-time teacher, a part-time writer, and the single parent of five adopted and foster children. She blogs and leads retreats and classes based on her program to develop habits to grow a joyful spirit. Her hobbies include tae kwon do, quilting, studying languages, and playing mahjong (badly).

Mary C. M. Phillips ("Air in My Tires" and "My Song, His Timing") is a musician and writer of short stories. She has toured nationally as a keyboardist and backup vocalist for various rock groups and musical comedy artists. She is blessed with a wonderful husband, son, and stepson and resides in New York.

Ellen Seibert Poole ("Fruitful or Fruitless?") is a freelance writer, a musician, and an occupational therapist on "creative sabbatical." Her published work includes articles and stories for magazines, newsletters, and compilation books. Formerly of Portland, Oregon, she and her husband, Harley, now reside in rural Southwest Washington, and are the proud parents of adult daughters Andrea and Erika.

JoAnne Potter ("Caught") is a retired teacher. During her twenty-five-year writing career, she has published nonfiction articles, a weekly column, reviews, and creative nonfiction. She is the mother of two grown sons and shares her home in the hills of rural Southwestern Wisconsin with David, her husband of thirty-two years.

Kathryn Thompson Presley ("Love Covers") is a retired English professor living in Bryan, Texas. A conference speaker and freelance writer, she has published about fifty stories and essays as well as a chapbook of poetry. She enjoys reading; teaching Women in the Word, her ladies' Bible class; and playing Scrabble with her grandchildren.

Susan E. Ramsden ("Mentoring Megan), writer, speaker, and retired teacher, lives with her husband, Howard, in Santa Maria, California. They are the parents of Kim and grandparents of Olivia and Luke. Susan enjoys encouraging others through her spiritual poetry, devotionals, and speaking engagements. Her work has been published in several editions of *Cup of Comfort*®.

Susan Kelly Skitt ("Jesus Took the Wheel") lives on a beautiful hillside in rural Pennsylvania with her husband and two sons. She loves to write about God's mercy, forgiveness, and grace.

Lissa Stressman Smith ("Necklace of Many Blessings") lives in Saugatuck, Michigan, with her husband, Rob, and her two dogs, Charles Dickens and John Steinbeck (a.k.a. Dickens and Steinee). She was employed for many years as a newspaper reporter and theater reviewer for Kaechele Publications and has been a grant writer for Christian Neighbors for the last thirteen years. Her work has appeared in *Hurricane Alice*, *Mobius*, and various local publications.

Helena Solano ("My Cross, His Cross") was born in Detroit, Michigan, into a large Mexican-American family. She holds a master's degree in counseling and a post-master's in school counseling. She lives with her two teenage children and husband in the Detroit area. Helena enjoys reading, writing, and being with her family.

Heather Spiva ("The Test of Tithe") is a freelance writer from Sacramento, California. She loves reading, writing, and spending time with her husband and two sons.

Diane Stark ("Bless the Weeds and the Children") is a former teacher turned stay-at-home mom and freelance writer. She writes about the important things in her life: her family and her faith. Her work has appeared in dozens of magazines and anthologies, and she is the author of *Teacher's Devotions to Go*. She lives in Brazil, Indiana, with her husband and their five children.

Joyce Stark ("A Sign from Above") retired from local government and is now a freelance writer living in Northeast Scotland. Joyce and her husband travel widely in the United States, and she writes travel articles for various journals. She has also written a series for young children, introducing them to a second language.

Renae Tolbert ("Divine Intervention") lives in Redding, California, where she enjoys photographing nature and wildlife. She has won several awards for her photos and has been published in *Birds & Blooms* magazine. In addition to writing and being a photographer, she enjoys hiking and mountain biking with her husband, Herb.

Nancy Tusinski ("It Is a Gift to Receive") works as a librarian in southeastern Vermont. Her poem "First Garden" won honorable mention in the fifth annual *Writer's Digest* Poetry Awards competition, and her prayer/poem "The Unquiet Ones" appears in the book *Lifting Women's Voices: Prayers to Change the World*.

Stefanie Wass ("Seeds of Friendship") writes from her home in Hudson, Ohio. As a freelance writer, her work has appeared in the *Los Angeles Times, Seattle Times, Christian Science Monitor, Cleveland Magazine, Akron Beacon Journal, Akron Life and Leisure*, and numerous anthologies. She is a member of SCBWI and is seeking representation for her middle grade novel.

Toianna Wika ("My Journey from Judgment to Love"), a freelance writer and editor, lives in St. Paul, Minnesota, with her husband and two children. She writes for several local publications, including the *Christian Chronicle*, is interested in writing young adult novels, and has begun a full-length novel based on Matthew 22:37–40.

About the Editor

COLLEEN SELL has compiled and edited thirty-six volumes of the *Cup of Comfort*® book series. A seasoned writer and editor, she has authored, ghostwritten, or edited more than one hundred additional books, served as editor-in-chief of two award-winning magazines, and had scores of her articles and essays published. She and her husband, T.N. Trudeau, share an ancient farmhouse on a forty-acre slice of heaven on earth in the Pacific Northwest.